Ovid: Metamorphoses III

Bloomsbury Latin Texts

Other titles in the series:

Ovid: Metamorphoses III

An Extract: 511–733

With introduction, commentary and vocabulary by

John Godwin

B L O O M S B U R Y
LONDON • NEW DELHI • NEW YORK • SYDNEY

Bloomsbury Academic

An imprint of Bloomsbury Publishing Plc

50 Bedford Square	1385 Broadway
London	New York
WC1B 3DP	NY 10018
UK	USA

www.bloomsbury.com

Bloomsbury is a registered trade mark of Bloomsbury Publishing Plc

First published 2014

Introduction, notes and vocabulary © John Godwin, 2014

British Library Cataloguing-in-Publication Data
A catalogue record for this book is available from the British Library.

ISBN: PB: 978-1-4725-0850-8
ePub: 978-1-4725-0807-2
ePDF: 978-1-4725-0776-1

Library of Congress Cataloging-in-Publication Data
Ovid, 43 B.C.-17 A.D. or 18 A.D., author.
Metamorphoses III : a selection: 511-733 / Ovid ; with introduction, commentary and vocabulary by John Godwin.
pages cm
Includes bibliographical references and index.
ISBN 978-1-4725-0850-8 (pbk. : alk. paper)– ISBN 978-1-4725-0807-2 (epub)– ISBN 978-1-4725-0776-1 (epdf) 1. Ovid, 43 B.C.-17 A.D. or 18 A.D. Metamorphoses. I. Godwin, John, 1955- II. Title.
PA6519.M4 G632014
873'.01–dc23
2013033628

Typeset by Fakenham Prepress, Fakenham, Norfolk, NR21 8NN
Printed and bound in Great Britain

Contents

Preface

This book is intended to assist students preparing for public examinations in Latin who are required to study this text, but it can of course be used by any students of Latin who have mastered the basics and who are now ready to start reading some Latin verse and developing their skills and their understanding. The notes assume that the reader has studied the Latin language roughly as far as GCSE, but the vocabulary list glosses every word in the text and the Introduction assumes that the reader is coming to Ovid for the very first time. The commentary seeks to elucidate the background and the literary features of this highly artistic text, while also helping the reader to understand how the Latin words fit together into their sentences.

My thanks are due above all to Charlotte Loveridge and Dhara Patel and their team at Bloomsbury who have been a model of efficiency and enthusiasm and a delight to write for. My thanks also go to Martin Thorpe and to Stephen Anderson who both read the whole of this book in draft form and made many highly useful comments which saved me from error as well as pointing me towards a better reading of the text. Professor Richard Tarrant of Harvard University was of great assistance with a knotty linguistic matter. All mistakes which remain are, of course, my own.

John Godwin, Shrewsbury
February 2013

Introduction

Why read this text?

The story

This is a short extract from a long poem, telling a grisly tale of an impious king getting his just deserts from an angry god. The tale is simple: King Pentheus of Thebes is outraged that his people are worshipping this strange god Bacchus and is determined to put a stop to their revelry – for Bacchus is the god of wine and various forms of ecstasy and his worship was uninhibited and must have been alarming to onlookers and rulers. The king sends his men to sort out these Bacchic worshippers but the men come back defeated. Along with them comes a stranger, Acoetes, with his own tale to tell. He had been on a voyage when they put into the shore for the night: his men find a young boy wandering around and decide to kidnap him for a ransom, despite Acoetes' demands that they do no such thing. The ship sets sail and suddenly the 'boy' turns out to be the god Bacchus himself who stops the ship with ivy growing up the oars and masts and then turns the sailors into dolphins. Acoetes warns King Pentheus to beware annoying this god – look what happened to my men when they tried a trick on him – but Pentheus takes no notice. He in fact gives orders for Acoetes to be tortured and killed for his impudence. The prisoner is miraculously set free, his chains slipping off his arms and the prison gates opening of their own accord. Pentheus is by now at the end of his tether and goes off to the mountainside to sort these Bacchants out himself once and for all. When he gets there he is spotted by his mother and her sisters who, in their divinely-induced hallucinatory trance, think he is a boar wandering on the grass and tear him limb from limb and rip his head clean off. After that the Thebans worship Bacchus and nobody would dare question this ever again.

The style

Ovid is a master of Latin verse. He manages to be subtle without being over-complex and his use of descriptive language and vivid dialogue brings the tale to life. Pentheus' speech urging the Thebans to stand up to this 'perfumed boy' is a classic of its kind: superbly constructed and yet obviously wrong-headed at the same time, a triumph of form over content. The passage in which the cheeky sailors are turned into dolphins is astonishing: the details of the transformation are packed in – their new skin and beaks, the loss of their arms etc. – and yet the tale does not drag and the whole crew is transformed within 15 lines. There is dramatic irony; we know full well that Pentheus is heading for disaster and yet we watch and listen to him blustering and refusing to see sense until it is too late.

The (amphi-)theatricality

This is a story which most people knew from going to the theatre: it had been put into tragedies in Greek and Latin and Ovid seems to allude to this several times: the use of Pentheus' big speech to outline the argument against Bacchus is typical of Greek tragedy, as is the use of the Messenger (in this case Acoetes) who warns the king of what has happened offstage. The dénouement is clearly dramatic and visual: indeed the setting on Mount Cithaeron is described as being a *spectabilis undique campus* – a plain open to view on all sides – which is a strong hint that we are in the position of a theatrical audience watching the awful fate unfold. What is worse, the actual events are more the stuff of the Roman amphitheatre than the Greek theatre as this spectacle enacts the brutal revenge on an impious king, the very Roman 'beast hunt' being enacted but (as in the case of Actaeon) with a human victim rather than the animal his killers supposed.

The 'message'?

This is of course highly problematic: we cannot now claim to know what Ovid intended when he composed this tale. It is clear, however, that a reading of this text explores a view of how we should behave, and how the gods in fact behave which will prompt discussion and argument. If gods behave like this – turning non-believers into dolphins or having them dismembered by their mothers – should we worship them? Equally, do we dare *not* worship beings powerful and callous enough to do this? The 'theology' of the tale is perhaps less important than the emotional investment of fear which the tale instils in the reader: this is a revenge drama told from the point of view of two cowed onlookers – the narrator and then the second narrator within the narrative, Acoetes.

Reading this story will not change your life – as reading Plato or Lucretius (for example) could. It will however give pleasure: the thrill of the horror story with the gory details in full colour on the page, the shiver of irony as the awful fate we can see coming hits the king (and the sailors) even more than we expected, the satisfaction of seeing bad behaviour rewarded with punishment but also the nagging doubt about the justification of this kind of 'moral'. The questions of 'sincerity' and 'intention' are still to be found in discussions of many writers, ancient and modern: Catullus' longest poem (64) ends with a 'moral' which may (or may not) be ironic, Juvenal appears to be pushing a hard line on social and moral issues but is doing so in the exaggerated manner of the satirist whose style undercuts the urge to take his words at face value, and so on. The fundamental 'purpose' of a writer is (of course) to write: and perhaps the one thing we can say with some measure of certainty about Ovid is that there is a delight in his own poetic and narrative skill which makes the poetry a constant source of pleasure and value in itself. The purpose of the commentary to this text is to begin the process of investigating the methods and the achievements of this most artistic of poets.

Ovid and his times

Publius Ovidius Naso was born on 20 March 43 BC in a small town called Sulmo (modern Sulmona) about 80 miles east of Rome. We know more about his upbringing than we do about that of other poets as he left a substantial body of autobiographical works, and he tells us that his family was well-off but not politically active. He was sent to school in Rome – one of the signs of wealth in an age where there was no free schooling – along with his brother, and he studied public speaking (with a view to a legal and/or political career) although he was more drawn to the writing of poetry than to the composition of speeches. He was born into turbulent times: by the time of his birth Julius Caesar had been dead almost a year and when he was 12 Caesar's great-nephew and heir Octavian defeated Mark Antony in the crucial battle off Actium, leaving the Roman world in the hands of a young man who was soon to change his name to Augustus and become the first of the emperors of Rome. The Roman republic which had stood ever since the last of the kings – the infamous Tarquinius Superbus – was expelled in 510 BC was now subverted into a 'Principate' in which supreme power rested in the hands of the *princeps* or emperor and freedom of speech and free elections came to be increasingly circumscribed and sanctioned. Ovid's choice of career as a writer rather than as a lawyer or politician (or both, as was Cicero) is therefore not totally surprising seeing that he was born in an age when the scope for a lively-minded man to find the outlet for his talents in politics was inevitably limited by the regime in power. Ovid hardly ever refers explicitly to politics in his works, although it is clear from some of his less guarded lines that he might not have survived long as a politician in the imperial court.

As a young man he did what we could call the Grand Tour, travelling to Greece, Sicily and Asia Minor, and it is clear from his work that he, like most educated Romans, understood and read Greek literature in the original. His training as a lawyer would have encouraged him to compose *suasoriae* – artificial exercises in which the student composes a speech to 'try to persuade' (*suadere*) a historical figure about to make some momentous act, such as Sulla about to invade Rome, or Hannibal after the Battle of Cannae. This sort of imaginative work did him no harm at all as a writer and his composition of speeches in particular shows ample signs of having been much influenced by these student exercises; Pentheus' speech to the Thebans in this book is just the kind of thing a young Ovid might have written in his rhetorical training.

Ovid's political career did not, then, last long and he soon devoted himself to writing poetry. He may have enjoyed the private means which other poets such as Horace did not have; or he may have continued with some business interests alongside his literary output. Literature was clearly however the focus of his career.

He began by writing love poetry in elegiac couplets: three books of *Amores* ('Loves', or 'Love-affairs') which are fully in the tradition of love-elegy. He published three books of these elegies, purporting to be love-poetry told in the first person: he followed this with the *Heroides*, which are fictional verse letters written from famous women of legend, such as Dido writing to Aeneas and Penelope to Ulysses.

Much of ancient literature was didactic in that it claimed to teach its readers lessons of one sort or another. Sometimes it was explicitly so, as in Nicander's poem *On Venomous Reptiles*, Lucretius' poem

De Rerum Natura or Virgil's *Georgics*, and sometimes it was simply a feeling that poetry 'ought' to educate young and old. Ovid next produced two works which pretended to be didactic literature, but composed them in the elegiac metre of love poetry rather than the hexameters of the traditional didactic epic. The *Medicamina Faciei Femineae* ('medical treatments for woman's appearance') looked at how women could maintain their appearance with drugs and potions – very much in the style of the didactic poet Nicander. We only have 100 lines surviving of this poem, but the *Ars Amatoria* (the first two books of which were published in 1 BC) was a sustained experiment in applying the form of didactic poetry to the elegiac content of the life of love, instructing young men how to court women using abundant material from literature and legend as well as some vivid descriptions of such features of ancient Rome as the Circus Maximus and its races. This was followed by the antidote to love (*Remedia Amoris* (1 BC–AD 2) which is clearly a sequel to the successful *Ars Amatoria*.

The *Metamorphoses* was written before his exile in AD 8 – an exile imposed on Ovid by the Emperor Augustus because of his unspecified poem (usually regarded as the *Ars Amatoria*) and his very mysterious 'crime' which seems to have consisted in the poet witnessing something secret and which was scandalous enough to have him banished to remote Tomis (modern Constanza on the Black Sea coast of Romania) for the rest of his life. Before his exile he had also begun to write the *Fasti* – poem on the feasts and tales associated with the Roman calendar, with one book for each of the months of the year.

Once stranded in exile in Tomis he composed the *Tristia* (AD 9–12) – 'sad things' – poems expressive of Ovid's misery in his banishment, as well as the *Epistulae ex Ponto* and the mysterious curse-poem *Ibis* (AD 10–11?). For all his poetic pleading, Ovid never returned to Rome and died at the age of 60 in AD 17.

Epic poetry and the *Metamorphoses*

Epic in the ancient world begins with Homer, whose *Iliad* and *Odyssey* – poems of enormous length composed in dactylic hexameters – framed the conventions of the genre for hundreds of years to come. Homer's poems concern themselves with warfare, heroism and gods and contain speeches and elaborate similes and this is very much what 'epic' meant to the ancient reader. Homer was imitated widely in the centuries after his death by writers such as Apollonius Rhodius (whose *Argonautica* we have) and many others whose works have not survived. The influential writer and critic Callimachus, who lived and worked in the great library at Alexandria in Egypt, led something of a revolt against the predominance of epic ('I detest epic' is one of his pithier fragments) and promoted the idea of literature as miniature gems of stylistic perfection rather than the broad brush of the epic narrative. His own surviving works show this tendency to give us the unexpected rather than to follow the well-trodden path of Homeric imitation, to produce small-scale poems rather than long tales – and Roman poets found themselves under the conflicting sways of both Homer and Callimachus. The last generation of the Roman republic saw the emergence of the so-called 'Neoteric' poets who followed the Callimachean aspiration of *l'art pour l'art* and produced such small-scale masterpieces as Catullus' short epic on Peleus and Thetis (poem 64). Then came Virgil.

Virgil's debt to Homer is obvious: the very opening words of his great Roman epic *The Aeneid* salute his Greek predecessor, with the *arma* of *arma virumque cano* representing the *Iliad* and the *virum* being a nod towards Odysseus who is the 'man' mentioned in the first word of Homer's *Odyssey*. Virgil's epic breaks into two halves, an 'Odyssean' (books 1–6) and an 'Iliadic' half (7–12) and the Roman poet's debt to Homer in terms of storyline, language and style are all immediately obvious. Clearly when Ovid decided to write his epic he was not going to try to imitate Virgil but needed to find his own way.

The result is the *Metamorphoses*, a continuous poem (*carmen perpetuum* as he calls it in *Metamorphoses* 1.4) in 15 books, containing roughly 250 tales of 'transformations' or 'shape-shifting'. Not for Ovid the concentrated narrative of the *Iliad*, dealing with a short period of time in the final year of the Trojan War, or the *Aeneid* with its constant movement in the direction of the foundation of Rome and its glorious future. Ovid's poem jumps from time to time and place to place, links between the stories being at times tenuous and keeping his readers on their toes by sometimes putting stories within other stories – as in this text where the tale of the sailors is embedded in the tale of Pentheus. Homer's *Iliad* is dominated by a theme – anger – and a small group of characters, whereas the *Metamorphoses* has a huge *dramatis personae* and defies easy analysis in thematic terms.

The obvious 'subject' of the poem is stated in its title – 'changes of shape' which is what the Greek word *metamorphosis* means. In the course of the poem we see people changed into animals (the sailors in this book become dolphins), trees (Baucis and Philemon), flowers (Narcissus), the opposite sex (Tiresias), stars (Julius Caesar) and even a god (Augustus' deification is prophesied in the final pages of book 15), and so on. This suits Ovid the writer perfectly as his blend of epic poetry and 'magic realism' is ideal for these tales of 'shape-shifting' which make up the poem. It also suits Ovid the literary stylist who can change one literary genre into another, so that disparate materials in a variety of forms – tragedy, comedy, elegy, lyric, rhetoric and so on – all find themselves metamorphosed into this highly sophisticated hexameter poetry. On the outside it all looks the same – but read the poem and you find yourself taken on something of a tour of ancient literature as well as a long voyage through the seas of myth and history. This also allows Ovid to indulge the ironic side of his writing. Kenneth Quinn once famously described Ovid as a *poseur* – which means a writer whose work pretends to be something which its ironic style denies, such as the ardent lover in the *Amores* or the 'teacher of love' in the *Ars Amatoria*. The *Metamorphoses* never allows the reader to become too emotionally involved in the feelings of the characters portrayed either because they are too bad to deserve our sympathy – just as Pentheus is here characterised as getting no more than a *contemptor superum* ('despiser of the gods') deserves – or else because they end up mysteriously better off – as in the case of the old couple Baucis and Philemon in book 8, who have their lifespan extended by several hundred years by being turned into adjoining trees, or (for that matter) in the case of the sailors here who are turned into apparently happy dolphins. There is also much comedy in the telling of the tales – for instance the cat-and-mouse game Bacchus plays on the sailors when he feigns fear and helplessness as he 'realises' that they are taking him away from Naxos, or the black humour of Pentheus trying to extend his arms in prayer to his mother only to find she has torn them off his body. The brilliance of the style sometimes impresses us so much that it gets in the way of our emotional involvement, even when the style is being used to persuade, as in the case of the rousing speech where Pentheus tries to instil patriotic fervour in his 'snake-born' Thebans by reminding them of their old foe the dragon, or in the wonderful 'messenger speech' piece of narrative when Acoetes tells the story of the sailors, or in the neat 'moral' ending to the book. This piece of Latin is skilful and versatile, and it shows Ovid the stylist at the height of his powers. The form is self-contained in a triptych A-B-A in which the tale of Pentheus begins the section and ends it, with a related middle section concerning Acoetes: this structure is exactly that of Catullus 64, which begins and ends with the marriage of Peleus and Thetis but has a lengthy middle section telling the tale of Ariadne being rescued by Bacchus after being abandoned on Naxos by Theseus, before ending with a moralistic coda. Ovid uses his art to display his art – in places such as his brilliant use of echoes in the

'Narcissus and Echo' section of book 3 or the highly entertaining 'catalogue' of Actaeon's dogs (206–25) which have significant names (such as 'Whitey', 'Blackey', 'Barker' and 'Shaggy') and this ironic manner makes Ovid a pleasure to read but has in the past made him seem a difficult poet to take seriously. Critics felt that he was just a clever wordsmith when compared to the gravity of a Virgil or a Homer. More recently, however, with the post-modernist emphasis on the textuality of literature and the self-conscious relationship all writers have with their work and the life it reflects, Ovid has come more into fashion, and his tales of shape-shifting no longer seem so silly in the age of 'magic realist' writers such as Gabriel Garcia Marquez and Jorge Luis Borges and television series such as *Heroes*.

Not that the events here described are themselves 'magic'. We only have Acoetes' word for the transformation of men into dolphins, and the murdering of a man by people in a state of madness is far from unknown in the 'real' world. The section ends with the Theban women, 'warned by examples such as these', inspired to make offerings to Bacchus now that his opponent Pentheus is safely dead. The writer rounds off the incident with a neat form of closure – 'that was what happened and so ever afterwards…' – but which focuses on the women of Thebes in order to lead straight into the start of book 4 and which leaves the tale on a sombre, fearful note. Ovid has in this extract covered his bases: his ending manages to distance the writer from the tale he has just told just as his use of direct speech from Acoetes resists any compulsion to pin the authority of Ovid himself to his tale, as does his subtle *fama est* in line 700.

Book 3

One of the features of the poem which has attracted a lot of critical attention is the way in which Ovid links his tales together into groups and some have seen book 3 as less coherent than it might have been in this respect. The link between the two tales here is obvious, as the tale of Acoetes and the sailors is linked to the 'frame-story' of Pentheus as (a) it is being narrated to Pentheus and so the speech is part of Pentheus' tale, and (b) it concerns the same god Bacchus and issues a warning about the way he should be regarded. The book as a whole, however, has less obvious links: it starts with the tale of Cadmus, founder of Thebes and the sower of dragon's teeth: the link to the next story is that one of Cadmus' grandsons was a hunter called Actaeon whose grisly death (in lines 141–252) is one of the most famous passages in the book. Actaeon accidentally saw the goddess Diana bathing naked and for this compromise to the modesty of the virgin goddess he is torn to pieces by his own hounds after he has been turned into a stag. This tale has obvious links with Pentheus – the insult to the god answered by the tearing of the miscreant to pieces, the crime being superficially one of seeing what should not be seen – but is quite different in other respects, as Actaeon was innocent of any blame whereas Pentheus was very much the architect of his own downfall. Both men were made to look like wild animals to be killed, but Pentheus' transformation is all in the deranged mind of his killers while Actaeon really did turn into the stag for the dogs to tear. Lines 253–315 tell the tale of Juno and Semele, where the jealous Juno tricks the gullible Semele (who is carrying Jupiter's child) into asking Jupiter to make love to her as he does with Juno, knowing that a mortal woman would never survive the experience. She is burnt to death in the ensuing conflagration, and Jupiter has to rescue his unborn son Bacchus from her womb and implant the child into his own thigh. The link with the previous tale is that Diana and Juno are both angry gods: the 'metamorphosis' is the change which Jupiter makes to his person to please the misguided Semele. The story of Semele is tragic in many ways – a woman in love who misguidedly incurs disaster, rather like Deianeira in Sophocles' *Women of Trachis* who also suffers for her mixture of love and naiveté – her 'mistake' being something like the *error* of the unwary Actaeon. The link with the tale of Pentheus is interesting. Clearly we see here the background of the god and can only pity this baby orphaned by the malice of a wicked stepmother, while at the same time it signals the ruthlessness of all gods – and Bacchus is a god – towards mortals.

Human tragedies do not touch the divine comedy, however, or not for long. In the next episode (316–510) there is a ludicrous debate between Jupiter and Juno about whether men or women enjoy sex more. They cannot agree and so they ask the expert Tiresias, who had been both male and female and so was competent to judge. He told them that women gain far more – 90 per cent in fact – of the pleasure, whereas men get a paltry 10 per cent of the fun. Jupiter was pleased with this answer which of course confirmed the male view that women were all incorrigibly and permanently randy and gave Tiresias prophetic gifts. Juno was angry and poked his eyes out. Tiresias was consulted about the future soon afterwards and one such consultation was about a young man called Narcissus – which leads to the tale of Narcissus and Echo. The debate between the gods about sex is shocking not least for the way it is sandwiched between the tragedy of Semele and the melodrama of Echo – another woman crucified by her helpless love who had already had the power of initiating speech taken from her by a jealous Juno and who now pined away with love until only her echoing voice remained, while the object of her affections Narcissus becomes a flower because he only loves himself and he is stuck to the adoring sight of his own reflection in a pool. The link here to the final (Pentheus) episode is the fame of Tiresias, who had so skilfully foreseen the fate of Narcissus, but who was despised by the arrogant King Pentheus who sneered at his blindness. This leads to the final section in which the king is killed for his impiety by his mother and the other Bacchants.

How do these tales make up a coherent narrative?

One common theme is that of changes of shape (metamorphosis):

- Actaeon is turned into a stag.
- Narcissus is turned into a flower.
- Echo is turned into a dismembodied voice.
- Sailors are turned into dolphins.
- Teeth are turned into soldiers.
- Jupiter is turned into mortal form to seduce Semele and then back to divine to kill her.
- Tiresias is turned into woman and then man again.
- Pentheus is not changed in fact – but his nearest and dearest are made not to recognise him as they kill him. The dogs see straight but Actaeon changes shape – Pentheus keeps his shape but the killers are deluded.

Another obvious link is avenging gods:

- Actaeon is punished by Diana for seeing her naked.
- Pentheus is punished by Bacchus for rejecting his deity.
- Tiresias is punished by Juno for giving the wrong answer.
- Semele is punished by Juno for bearing Jupiter's child.
- The sailors are punished by Bacchus for kidnapping him.
- Echo is punished by Juno for protecting Jupiter's lovers.
- Narcissus is punished for his spurning of lovers by Nemesis.

Less obviously, the theme is one of sexual love:

- Actaeon mistakenly compromises the virgin goddess Diana sexually.
- Semele loves Jupiter, but Juno also loves him and Juno's jealous love is the undoing of Semele and Echo, through their own loves (Semele for Jupiter, Echo for Narcissus).
- Narcissus loves himself and is cursed by a nameless *aliquis* (404) into self-destruction at the hands of Nemesis.

- Tiresias suffers the loss of his eyesight for the 'war of the sexes' in the ludicrous debate on the pleasures of sex.
- Pentheus would seem to be an exception to this – but in the Euripidean version of the tale he is presented as a repressed repressor of what he sees as the sexual misconduct of the Bacchants, and so perhaps Ovid puts him into this book for that reason.

Note however that, for all their common themes, the stories do not pursue a monotonous moral tone. Some characters are to blame for pride/stupidity (Pentheus, sailors, Narcissus); others are helpless victims of their own overpowering emotions (Semele, Echo); and others blameless (Actaeon – 'for how could a mistake be a crime?' *quid enim scelus error habebat?* 142). Divine retribution falls on the deserving and on the undeserving, and the contrast between the tragedy on earth and the levity of the gods' attitude towards it is brought out sharply in the contrast between the death of Semele and the farcical divine conversation which follows it.

Above all, think of the literary effects of this book. Ovid avoids tedium in his writing by constantly shifting the tone and the emphasis from narrative to rhetoric, tragedy to farce, gods to men, land to sea. In the Narcissus/Echo episode, for instance, he shows a real interest in psychology, somewhat like the analysis of Medea in Apollonius Rhodius' *Argonautica*, and manages to make Echo's story more plausible as her obsessive love ends up being self-destructive. On the surface this is a simple tale of Juno punishing a cheeky nymph by making her love the unattainable, killing two birds with one curse by having the unattainable destroyed by his own self-infatuation, but Ovid invests far more subtlety in the tale and Echo's wasting away is a convincing portrayal of a woman in emotional turmoil.

In the Pentheus tale there is a similar simplicity about the moral of the text: right at the start we are told that Pentheus was a *contemptor superum* and that he mocked the old man Tiresias, just as the greedy sailors abuse and mock poor Acoetes who is trying to protect the innocent 'boy'. Pride goes before a fall, and just as in the case of Narcissus, Pentheus will suffer for his arrogance. Notice however the subtlety of the story: the irony (or poetic justice) of Pentheus being both produced and destroyed through his mother, the dramatic irony of his dismissing of Bacchus as a mere youth (553) and the rhetoric he comes up with to instil martial valour into the 'offspring of Mars' (531), the irony that Pentheus' 'madness' (*rabies*) makes him go to the mountain where the real madness of his mother and her sisters is waiting for him. Just as Narcissus suffered the Tantalus-style torment of seeing his beloved reflection recede from him whenever he reached out to it, so also Pentheus speaks to and pleads with his mother and his aunt (he even uses the title *matertera* ('auntie'); 79) but they cannot recognise him and ignore his words. Pentheus' last words (725) could not be more appropriate – 'look, mother' – as looking is what cost him his life as Tiresias predicted (517–18) and the poignancy of the son pleading with a murderous mother is highly charged, a sentiment which in other contexts (such as the tale of Medea for instance) could have been tragic but which here is made into almost sick humour as he waves his armless shoulders at her, the deluded son now seeing straight and the deluded mother unaware of who he is, shouting her victorious claim 'our work is now our victory' (728). The virtuosity of the narrative makes the horrific events both vivid and stylised, witty and ghastly at the same time: the (amphi-)theatrical scene-setting in the clearing giving a good view for Pentheus (and for us the audience) setting up the suspense, followed by the immediate act of seeing emphasised by the tricolon of *prima ... prima ... prima* (711–12), the direct speech of Agaue with hyperbaton showing her disordered state of mind and repeated *ille* suggesting her pointing out the 'beast' (713–15), the neat ring-composition whereby Pentheus mentions his cousin Actaeon (720–1) to remind his aunt of who he is and which also reminds the reader of the earlier tale of a man who incurred the wrath of a god. Ovid's delight in verbal fireworks is most obvious in the transformation of the sailors into dolphins as he savours (678) the transformation of 'hands' into 'fins' (*manus* into *pinnas*), the speed of the metamorphosis being brought out in the near juxtaposition of the two words in the line; another sailor was keen to grasp the plaited ropes and there is a whole line expressing this wish (679) before the sudden truth hits in three words: *bracchia non habuit* (680). The two tales (of Pentheus and of Acoetes) mirror each other, as each of them ends with the survivors worshipping Bacchus (690–1, 732–3). There are also the familiar rhetorical tricks running through the piece such as the anaphoras (e.g. 539, 632–3), chiasmus at 611–12 and 655, the rhetorical 'deliberative' question (538), the homely touch of Acoetes' poor childhood with his worthy but impecunious father (582–91), the detailed knowledge of stars shown by Acoetes with five proper names mentioned in two lines (594–5) showing that he really does know what he is talking about, the amusingly inappropriate names given to some of the sailors ('Melanthus' ('black-flower') is *flavus*; 617) and above all the in-jokes in places such as 608–9, where the god of wine seems to be drunk, or the ironic threat in 579–80 where the words of Pentheus to Acoetes ('by your death you will give lessons to others') will in fact apply to him rather than to his victim, or the way in which the sailors accuse Acoetes of being mad (641) when it is they who are not seeing the truth. Ovid uses the metre expressively, such as the sluggish spondees in line 662 when they are trying and failing to move the ship, and his sound-effects are easily spotted by anyone who reads this poetry aloud – look for instance at the ringing sounds of the bacchants in the alliteration and assonance of lines 702–3:

> *Cithaeron*
> *cantibus et clara bacchantum voce sonabat*

All ancient poetry was written to be recited aloud, of course, and there is much to be gained from hearing this text spoken to appreciate the effects of the metre and the verbal sound-effects which the poet so skilfully embeds in his text; the commentary points out many of these but there are many others which readers can discover for themselves and which must have been instrumental in making the performance of the work impressive to its audience.

The epic poet always uses similes, but the ones in this text are short and straight to the point (e.g. Pentheus was inspired like a horse hearing the trumpet going to battle (704–5)), unlike the extended similes we find in Homer, and often the similes amount to a tiny thumbnail sketch such as the dolphins 'looking like a chorus' (685). The poet composes speeches to put into the mouth of his main heroes (Tiresias, Pentheus and Acoetes) and all of these are appropriate to the character. Tiresias speaks in a suitably oracular style (*auguror*; 519) and uses inflated grammatical forms such as *fueris dignatus* (521: for *eris dignatus*) along with his confident prophetic future indicatives (*spargere, foedabis, eveniet*) to give Pentheus the lessons he needs but will reject. Pentheus speaks with a suitable mixture of patriotism (calling the Thebans' attention to their ancestry and their past valour in line 531) and mockery of the enemy they now face (this unarmed boy) using the argument form *a fortiori*:

> You defeated the dragon before
> This enemy is far less fierce than the dragon was
> Therefore you will easily defeat this enemy if you try to.

Only towards the end of this speech do we see the king's sense of his own weak position when he contrasts himself with Acrisius and refers to himself in the pompous third-person:

> *Penthea terrebit cum totis advena Thebis?*
> ('Will the stranger terrify Pentheus along with all of Thebes?')

The fear mentioned in *terrebit* is actually inside Pentheus who sees power being taken from him as he has lost control over his people:

and his fear turns (as fear often does) into cruelty towards Bacchus and later on towards Acoetes. Acoetes is brought in arrested with his arms tied behind his back, reminiscent in this of Sinon in Virgil's *Aeneid* 2 who is also brought in to tell a tale which will have disastrous effects on its hearers. He seems oddly unconcerned (*metu vacuus*; 582) and takes his time telling a long tale (Pentheus later describes his speech as 'rambling'; 692) to show the king what this stranger can do. Here again we have direct speech quoted inside the direct speech of Acoetes' tale, we have some very strong action – such as Acoetes getting punched in the throat by Lycabas (626–7) – and we have some wonderful narrative art shown in the transformation first of the ship, then of the men, with the side-show of the tigers, lynxes and panthers thrown in for extra effect. Ovid writes a speech for each character which seems to come straight from the speaker's heart; but he also manages to convey dialogue in reported speech (572–3):

> *Bacchus ubi esset*
> *quaerenti domino Bacchum vidisse negarunt*

This amounts to:

> ' "where is Bacchus?"
> The master asked. 'We have not seen Bacchus' they said.'

The closing section of the book is remarkable for the way Ovid does *not* take the opportunity to investigate the 'psychopathology' of Pentheus as Euripides had done in the *Bacchae*. Pentheus here is simply the 'despiser of the gods' who rejects the old prophet and the god with the same dismissive scepticism. This makes the narrative unusually 'conventional' with minatory prophecies presaging the end and a set-piece description of the slaughter, the moral being drawn by Acoetes and the closing lines of the book which see the incident as an *exemplum* conveying a moral message. Is this Ovid reverting to the banal? Or is it ironic?

One of the cardinal features of Alexandrian literature was the stress on novelty of treatment in its handling of a literary *topos* (set theme). Instead of trotting out the old story in the familiar manner, the poet tried to find a new way to look at it, rather as later Greek sculptures which were made to be seen from several different angles as well as the four-square front view. So the 'modern' Euripidean view of Pentheus was perhaps less attractive for Ovid precisely because it had been done so successfully already. Paradoxically, the more 'primitive' account of Pentheus would be more original; and yet the writer is still interested in psychopathology. This time it is that of the women hallucinating and murdering their own rather than the crazed king of Euripides.

Bacchus

The god whom the Romans called Bacchus or Liber was the equivalent of the Greek god Dionysus and was one of the most interesting of the ancient deities, as well as one of the more complex. Born, as Ovid tells us, from the thigh of his father Jupiter after the death of his mother Semele, and brought up initially by nymphs on Mount Nysa, he is a mixture of god and man; and his image depicts him also as a mixture of young and old, man and animal, male and female, able to appear at will and work miracles when his quixotic mind wanted to do so, and constantly on the move. He induced in his followers a state of trance-like ecstasy which enabled them to perform amazing feats themselves such as the dismemberment of a king in the passage in this book, holding of snakes in their hands, etc. He was linked to wine and intoxication, but is also the god of the theatre – perhaps because both wine and drama take people (actors and audience) out of their inhibited selves and enable them to become somebody new. He is described in Euripides' *Bacchae* 861 as 'most terrible and yet

most sweet to mortals' and his depiction in Ovid bears this out well
– he is irresistibly attractive to the crowd of Thebans who rush out
to worship him and his image in Acoetes' tale is that of a harmless
young boy, and yet he wrecks the lives of those who cross him. The
wine which he represents and embodies is itself a mixed blessing of
course, but images of him on vases from the classical period show
him as the ultimate party animal, surrounded by his followers the
satyrs (the animalistic beings who are permanently seeking wine and
sex), nymphs (beautiful female nature-spirits) and the Maenads.

These Maenads were mortal women who would go up to the
mountains in the depths of winter to worship the god. They would
remove their shoes, let down their hair and start to dance, accompanied
by the drum and the pipe and in the glimmer of torchlight, until they
fell into a state of ecstatic trance. The legends have it that in this state
of trance they were insensitive to pain – and obviously to cold – and
that they tore animals apart with their bare hands and ate the meat raw.
There is little hard evidence for this – and some revisionist attempts
have been made to show the Maenads as engaging in a more prosaic
social and religious event on the mountain away from their menfolk.

Drink is of course an inescapable part of the myth of Dionysus:
Odysseus tells the incredulous Polyphemus in Euripides' play *Cyclops*
(519–28) that the wine-skin has a god living in it. Yet the rituals and
the ecstasies do not seem to have been driven by alcohol, and the
worshippers did not think of themselves as either mad or intoxicated
but simply in the hands of the god. It is interesting that Ovid uses
the name *Liber* often in preference to *Bacchus* – even in lines such as
528 where *Bacchus* would have fitted the metre perfectly – and there
is almost a sense in these early lines in the passage that the god is a
'liberator' of the Thebans from the repressive regime of Pentheus,
with the god giving them a holiday (*festis*; 528) in which all social
classes and ages mix freely in a happy throng – although the dark side
is hinted at in *fremunt ululatibus* which looks forward to Pentheus'

marching out to face the Bacchants in 704–6 where similar language is used.

Dionysus has been seen in European thought – especially in the works of such thinkers as Nietzsche – as the embodiment of that fertile chaos, the irrational 'dark' side of humanity as opposed to Apollo the sun-god and the bringer of healing and light. His worship shows human beings losing their self-control and acting in ways which to outsiders seemed mad and subversive to the good order of the state. Dionysus' birthplace was Thebes and it is only natural that this city became the home of Maenadism. It is also unsurprising that a king who was keen to maintain tight control over the people in his city would be unimpressed when they ran off to worship this ambivalent and unsettling god. Drama feeds on conflict, and the clash between the political ruler and the divine being was always going to make good drama. There was also good Roman relevance in the story: the Roman Senate had taken steps to ban the Bacchic rites from Rome in 186 BC, and Livy tells us that so long as the cult was confined to women the Senate had few objections; it was only when a new priestess started to initiate men (cf. the note to lines 529–30) that the Senate feared the practices would make Roman men effeminate and therefore unfit to be citizens (Livy 39.15.9–14) – sentiments which Ovid puts into the mouth of Pentheus (see note on line 547).

Pentheus

The name Pentheus derives from the Greek word *penthos* meaning 'sorrow' or 'pain' and it was always obvious that the fight between him and the god would end painfully for the king; Ovid adds to this theme by making Pentheus the sadistic ruler who also *inflicts* pain such as the unnecessary torture of Acoetes in lines 694–8. The traditional tale sees Pentheus as a young king faced with a mysterious stranger who

is in fact Dionysus/Bacchus in human form but whom Pentheus sees
as merely a bad influence on the good women of Thebes. The king
imprisons the stranger – only for him to burst out of his prison when
an earthquake knocks its walls down. The god now bewitches the
king somehow and gets him to dress up as a woman and go to Mount
Cithaeron to spy on the women; when they get to the mountain the
women then think the man is a wild beast and kill him. His mother
Agaue brings home Pentheus' head in triumph, telling everyone that it
is the head of a lion she has killed; her father Cadmus has the sad duty
of bringing her to her senses and letting her see what she has done.
The story was told most famously in Euripides' play *The Bacchae* but
was also handled by Aeschylus and other Greek tragedians and was
adapted into Latin in tragedies by Accius and Pacuvius of which only
fragments survive. The difference between the Euripidean version of
the tale and that in Ovid is however marked. Euripides has Pentheus
influenced directly by the god in his desire to go and spy on the
women, whereas Ovid simply has Pentheus march out as an irate
king fed up with all this prevarication. The psychological subtlety
of the tragedy – the voyeurism, the cross-dressing and so on – are
all missing from Ovid's simpler tale of pride being punished, of a
king eager to rule being himself murdered by his subjects and of a
god proving his divinity by the harshest of lessons. Closer perhaps
to Ovid is the tale as told in the Hellenistic poet Theocritus' 26th
Idyll, composed about 270 BC also in hexameters: Theocritus has
Ino, Autonoe and Agaue leading three groups of Maenads to the
mountain and seeing Pentheus watching their secret rituals.

> By now she was in a frenzy as were the others and they chased him:
> Pentheus spoke thus: 'what do you want, women?'
> Autonoe said this: 'you will soon know before you even hear it.'
> His mother grabbed her son's head and roared
> Like the roar of a lioness with cubs.
> Ino tore off the great shoulder along with the shoulder-blade

Stepping with her feet on his stomach, and Autonoe did the same
    sort of thing:
The remaining bits of him the other women butchered up
And they all came to Thebes spattered with blood
Bringing from the mountain not Pentheus but penthea (pain)...(12–26)

This is close to Ovid but is (again) not the sole model for the Roman poet and the differences are also plain: Ovid does not actually show the mother ripping off the head for one thing (although he strongly suggests it in lines 725–8) and is more interested in how Pentheus spoke and how Agaue looked than he is in the butchery itself.

The character of Pentheus in Ovid is less subtle perhaps than we had expected. He is full of anger and spirit – what the Greeks termed *thymos* – and he can compose a calculated speech targeting different groups of his audience with reminders of their glorious past and taunting them with their imminent defeat by a bunch of weaklings (*molles*; 547) led by a perfumed boy. When he is opposed his 'rage/madness' (*rabies*) only grows all the more and this is to some extent a stock feature of tyrants and leaders in ancient literature – from Achilles dragging the corpse of his dead foe Hector round the tomb of Patroclus in Homer's *Iliad* to Xerxes flogging the Hellespont (Herodotus 7.34) to Oedipus' famously short fuse when faced with the unco-operative Tiresias in Sophocles' *Oedipus the King*.

In Euripides' *Bacchae* the king's motive for going to the mountain was to spy on these women rather than simply to kill them as here; Euripides has him being led to wear women's clothing to escape notice and yet there is also a strong sense that this is the god undermining the macho side of the blustering king by 'feminising' him, but Ovid resists this whole side of the encounter and merely has Pentheus marching out for himself once his servants have tried to arrest Bacchus and failed bloodily. The death of the king is a study in revenge from the god to the ruler who is no longer talking big (717) but who is now pleading with his mother and aunt like a child.

Acoetes

Acoetes is not in Euripides' *Bacchae* where the stranger before the
king is the god himself in disguise. It is tempting to at least wonder
whether Acoetes is the god himself (who is a master of disguise), as
Pentheus had ordered his men to bring the *ducem* in chains (562–3)
and this would give more point to his remark (658–9):

> *Nec enim praesentior illo/ est deus.*
> ('No god is more present than that one'.)

It would be typical of Bacchus to fool Pentheus in this way – but it
is also typical of Ovid to foil the reader's expectations and not to
do the obvious but to leave his audience guessing. The tale which
Acoetes tells does (after all) remind us of the many 'Lying Tales'
which Odysseus tells in the course of the *Odyssey* and which always
start with a (false) name and address just like lines 582–3. It also
adds a very lively metamorphosis (of men turned into dolphins) to
Pentheus' tale, which is otherwise lacking one.

The tale of the wicked sailors who try to take Bacchus hostage and
who are punished goes back a long way, however. The seventh *Homeric
Hymn* describes how the god 'like a young man in first manhood' was
walking on the shore, when Etruscan sailors captured him and bound
him onboard their ship only to find that the fetters fell off him. The
(unnamed) helmsman at once realised that this was no ordinary
hostage but one of the gods, and shouted at them to let the youth go.
The captain would not listen and tried to set sail at once; but the ship
was overwhelmed with gushing wine, a vine grew along the top of
the sail and ivy grew about the mast, forming berries and garlands.
The young man now became a lion in the ship and a shaggy-maned
bear elsewhere in the vessel. The lion seized the impious captain and
the crew leapt into the sea and turned into dolphins. The helmsman
was not punished as he alone had respected the god. This is so close

to Ovid that it is possible that there was a common source for both tales, and there is a well-known vase-painting by Exekias from about 530 BC which shows Dionysus/Bacchus reclining on a ship with vines growing on the mast and dolphins swimming in the sea around it which might also reflect the tale.

The metre of the poem

Latin poetry is written in a fairly rigid system of metres, all of which in turn rely on the pattern of heavy and light syllables, and the metre of the *Metamorphoses* is the 'hexameter', which is a line of six feet. The first four of these 'feet' can be either 'dactyls' (–∪∪) or 'spondees' (––), where the symbol '–' indicates a heavy syllable and the symbol '∪' a light one. It is usually assumed that a heavy syllable is equivalent to two light ones. The fifth foot of a hexameter is almost always a dactyl (line 669 is the exception in this passage) and the final foot is always one of two syllables, and so it is either a spondee or else a trochee (–∪).

Syllables which contain a diphthong (i.e., a pair of vowels pronounced together such as *au, ae*) or else a long vowel are heavy syllables, and syllables where a short vowel is followed by two (or more) consonants are also made heavy – although if the second consonant is 'l' or 'r' (such as in the word *patris*) then this need not happen. The two consonants do not have to be in the same word as the vowel for this to take place (e.g. 705: *dedit tubicen* where the (short) final 'i' of *dedit* is followed by t+t and so lengthened).

Single vowels may be long or short by nature and may vary with inflection (e.g. the final -*a* of *mensa* is long by nature in the ablative case, short in the nominative) and one must be aware that the letter 'i' may be a vowel in some places (*nix*) and a consonant in others (*iam*). The quantity of vowels is marked with a '–' symbol in good dictionaries such as James Morwood's *Pocket Oxford Latin Dictionary* (Oxford University Press, 2005).

In cases where a word ending with a vowel (or a vowel + m such as *iustam*) is followed by a word beginning with a vowel or *h*, the two syllables usually merge ('elide') into a single syllable, as *ubi electus* (702) is scanned as *ub'electus* (four syllables).

Thus a 'typical' hexameter line will run:

–∪∪/ –∪∪ /– //– / –∪∪ / –∪∪ / – –
út fremit/ ácer equ/ús, // cum/ béllicus/ áere so/nóro

where the ´ sign indicates the stressed syllable at the beginning of a foot and the // sign shows the 'caesura' – the word-break in the middle of a foot within the line. This usually happens in the third foot after the initial heavy syllable but can also come in the middle of the two short syllables in a dactyl, where it is usually accompanied by a caesura in the fourth foot, as in line 715:

ille mihi feriendus// aper// ruit omnis in unum

or lines 588, 602 and 733.

Latin words also have a natural stress accent (which works as in the same way as English words such as táble, spectátor, fúrniture), whereby most words were stressed on the penultimate syllable, or on the antepenultimate if the penultimate were a short vowel. Thus the final line of the book would be spoken:

Túraque dánt sánctasque cólunt Isménides áras

but 'scanned' metrically as:

Túraque dánt sanctásque colúnt Isménides áras

Quite how the two ways of reading Latin verse blended or competed is unclear: one notes that in hexameters there is a tendency for the stress accent and the metrical ictus to collide in the earlier and middle parts of the line but to coincide at the end – a tendency which is however abruptly broken when the line ends with a monosyllable as at 627 where the line ends with Acoetes' breathless *si non*.

Further reading

The most accessible translations of the whole of the *Metamorphoses* are those in the Penguin Classics series by David Raeburn (London, 2004) or else in the Oxford World Classics series by A. D. Melville (Oxford, 2008).

There is an edition of the whole of book 3 by A. A. R. Henderson in the same series as this book (Bristol Classical Press, 1981), and also a good (if brief) edition (with a facing English translation) of books 1–4 of the *Metamorphoses* by D. E. Hill (Oxbow Books, 1985)

For general books on the *Metamorphoses* see:

Fantham, E. (2004), *Ovid's Metamorphoses*, London.
Feldherr, A. (2010), *Playing Gods: Ovid's Metamorphoses and the Politics of Fiction*, Princeton.
Galinsky, K. (1975), *Ovid's Metamorphoses: an Introduction to the Basic Aspects*, Oxford.
Janan, M. (2009), *Reflections in a Serpent's Eye*, Oxford.
Otis, B. (1996), *Ovid as an Epic Poet*, Cambridge.

For more general discussions of Ovid see:

Hardie, P. (ed.) (2002), *The Cambridge Guide to Ovid*, Cambridge.
—(2007), *Ovid's Poetics of Illusion*, Cambridge.
Wilkinson, L. P. (1955), *Ovid Recalled*, Cambridge.

For a brief guide to the scansion of Latin hexameter poetry see:

Kennedy, B. H. (1962), *The Revised Latin Primer*, London, pp. 204–5.

Text

cognita res meritam vati per Achaidas urbes
attulerat famam, nomenque erat auguris ingens.
spernit Echionides tamen hunc ex omnibus unus
contemptor superum Pentheus praesagaque ridet
verba senis tenebrasque et cladem lucis ademptae   515
obicit. ille movens albentia tempora canis
'quam felix esses, si tu quoque luminis huius
orbus' ait 'fieres, ne Bacchica sacra videres.
namque dies aderit, quam non procul auguror esse,
qua novus huc veniat, proles Semeleia, Liber,   520
quem nisi templorum fueris dignatus honore,
mille lacer spargere locis et sanguine silvas
foedabis matremque tuam matrisque sorores.
eveniet; neque enim dignabere numen honore,
meque sub his tenebris nimium vidisse quereris.'   525
talia dicentem proturbat Echione natus.

dicta fides sequitur, responsaque vatis aguntur.
Liber adest, festisque fremunt ululatibus agri:
turba ruit, mixtaeque viris matresque nurusque
vulgusque proceresque ignota ad sacra feruntur.   530
'quis furor, anguigenae, proles Mavortia, vestras
attonuit mentes?' Pentheus ait; 'aerane tantum
aere repulsa valent et adunco tibia cornu
et magicae fraudes, ut, quos non bellicus ensis,
non tuba terruerit, non strictis agmina telis,   535
femineae voces et mota insania vino
obscenique greges et inania tympana vincant?
vosne, senes, mirer, qui longa per aequora vecti
hac Tyron, hac profugos posuistis sede penates,
nunc sinitis sine Marte capi? vosne, acrior aetas,   540
o iuvenes, propiorque meae, quos arma tenere,
non thyrsos, galeaque tegi, non fronde, decebat?
este, precor, memores, qua sitis stirpe creati,

illiusque animos, qui multos perdidit unus,
sumite serpentis. pro fontibus ille lacuque   545
interiit: at vos pro fama vincite vestra.
ille dedit leto fortes: vos pellite molles
et patrium retinete decus. si fata vetabant
stare diu Thebas, utinam tormenta virique
moenia diruerent, ferrumque ignisque sonarent.   550
essemus miseri sine crimine, sorsque querenda,
non celanda foret, lacrimaeque pudore carerent.
at nunc a puero Thebae capientur inermi,
quem neque bella iuvant nec tela nec usus equorum,
sed madidus murra crinis mollesque coronae   555
purpuraque et pictis intextum vestibus aurum,
quem quidem ego actutum (modo vos absistite) cogam
assumptumque patrem commentaque sacra fateri.
an satis Acrisio est animi, contemnere vanum
numen et Argolicas venienti claudere portas,   560
Penthea terrebit cum totis advena Thebis?
ite citi' (famulis hoc imperat), 'ite ducemque
attrahite huc vinctum. iussis mora segnis abesto.'
hunc avus, hunc Athamas, hunc cetera turba suorum
corripiunt dictis frustraque inhibere laborant.   565
acrior admonitu est irritaturque retenta
et crescit rabies moderaminaque ipsa nocebant.
sic ego torrentem, qua nil obstabat eunti,
lenius et modico strepitu decurrere vidi;
at quacumque trabes obstructaque saxa tenebant,   570
spumeus et fervens et ab obice saevior ibat.
ecce cruentati redeunt et, Bacchus ubi esset,
quaerenti domino Bacchum vidisse negarunt.
'hunc' dixere 'tamen comitem famulumque sacrorum
cepimus' et tradunt manibus post terga ligatis   575
sacra dei quendam Tyrrhena gente secutum.
aspicit hunc Pentheus oculis, quos ira tremendos
fecerat, et quamquam poenae vix tempora differt,
'o periture tuaque aliis documenta dature

morte, ait, 'ede tuum nomen nomenque parentum   580
et patriam, morisque novi cur sacra frequentes.'
ille metu vacuus 'nomen mihi' dixit 'Acoetes,
patria Maeonia est, humili de plebe parentes.
non mihi quae duri colerent pater arva iuvenci,
lanigerosve greges, non ulla armenta reliquit.   585
pauper et ipse fuit linoque solebat et hamis
decipere et calamo salientes ducere pisces.
ars illi sua census erat; cum traderet artem,
"accipe, quas habeo, studii successor et heres,"
dixit "opes", moriensque mihi nihil ille reliquit   590
praeter aquas: unum hoc possum appellare paternum.
mox ego, ne scopulis haererem semper in isdem,
addidici regimen dextra moderante carinae
flectere et Oleniae sidus pluviale Capellae
Taygetenque Hyadasque oculis Arctonque notavi   595
ventorumque domos et portus puppibus aptos.
forte petens Delum Chiae telluris ad oras
applicor et dextris adducor litora remis
doque leves saltus udaeque inmittor harenae.
nox ibi consumpta est. Aurora rubescere primo   600
coeperat; exsurgo laticesque inferre recentes
admoneo monstroque viam, quae ducat ad undas.
ipse quid aura mihi tumulo promittat ab alto
prospicio comitesque voco repetoque carinam.
"adsumus en" inquit sociorum primus Opheltes,   605
utque putat, praedam deserto nactus in agro,
virginea puerum ducit per litora forma.
ille mero somnoque gravis titubare videtur
vixque sequi; specto cultum faciemque gradumque:
nil ibi, quod credi posset mortale, videbam.   610
et sensi et dixi sociis: "quod numen in isto
corpore sit, dubito; sed corpore numen in isto est!
quisquis es, o faveas nostrisque laboribus adsis.
his quoque des veniam!" "pro nobis mitte precari!"
Dictys ait, quo non alius conscendere summas   615

ocior antemnas prensoque rudente relabi.
hoc Libys, hoc flavus, prorae tutela, Melanthus,
hoc probat Alcimedon et, qui requiemque modumque
voce dabat remis, animorum hortator, Epopeus,
hoc omnes alii; praedae tam caeca cupido est.   620
"non tamen hanc sacro violari pondere pinum
perpetiar" dixi: "pars hic mihi maxima iuris",
inque aditu obsisto. furit audacissimus omni
de numero Lycabas, qui Tusca pulsus ab urbe
exilium dira poenam pro caede luebat.   625
is mihi, dum resto, iuvenali guttura pugno
rupit et excussum misisset in aequora, si non
haesissem, quamvis amens, in fune retentus.
impia turba probat factum. tum denique Bacchus
(Bacchus enim fuerat), veluti clamore solutus   630
sit sopor aque mero redeant in pectora sensus,
"quid facitis? quis clamor?" ait "qua, dicite, nautae,
huc ope perveni? quo me deferre paratis?"
"pone metum" Proreus, "et quos contingere portus
ede velis!" dixit; "terra sistere petita."   635
"Naxon" ait Liber "cursus advertite vestros.
illa mihi domus est, vobis erit hospita tellus."
per mare fallaces perque omnia numina iurant
sic fore meque iubent pictae dare vela carinae.
dextera Naxos erat; dextra mihi lintea danti   640
"quid facis, o demens? quis te furor," inquit "Acoete,"
pro se quisque, "tenet? laevam pete." maxima nutu
pars mihi significat, pars quid velit aure susurrat.
obstipui "capiat" que "aliquis moderamina" dixi
meque ministerio scelerisque artisque removi.   645
increpor a cunctis, totumque inmurmurat agmen;
e quibus Aethalion "te scilicet omnis in uno
nostra salus posita est" ait et subit ipse meumque
explet opus Naxoque petit diversa relicta.
tum deus illudens, tamquam modo denique fraudem   650
senserit, e puppi pontum prospectat adunca

et flenti similis "non haec mihi litora, nautae,
promisistis" ait, "non haec mihi terra rogata est.
quo merui poenam facto? quae gloria vestra est,
si puerum iuvenes, si multi fallitis unum?"   655
iamdudum flebam: lacrimas manus impia nostras
ridet et impellit properantibus aequora remis.
per tibi nunc ipsum (nec enim praesentior illo
est deus) adiuro, tam me tibi vera referre
quam veri maiora fide: stetit aequore puppis   660
haud aliter, quam si siccum navale teneret.
illi admirantes remorum in verbere perstant
velaque deducunt geminaque ope currere temptant.
impediunt hederae remos nexuque recurvo
serpunt et gravidis distinguunt vela corymbis.   665
ipse racemiferis frontem circumdatus uvis
pampineis agitat velatam frondibus hastam;
quem circa tigres simulacraque inania lyncum
pictarumque iacent fera corpora pantherarum.
exsiluere viri, sive hoc insania fecit   670
sive timor, primusque Medon nigrescere coepit
corpore et expresso spinae curvamine flecti.
incipit huic Lycabas: "in quae miracula" dixit
"verteris?" et lati rictus et panda loquenti
naris erat, squamamque cutis durata trahebat.   675
at Libys obstantes dum vult obvertere remos,
in spatium resilire manus breve vidit et illas
iam non esse manus, iam pinnas posse vocari.
alter ad intortos cupiens dare bracchia funes
bracchia non habuit truncoque repandus in undas   680
corpore desiluit: falcata novissima cauda est,
qualia dimidiae sinuantur cornua lunae.
undique dant saltus multaque aspergine rorant
emerguntque iterum redeuntque sub aequora rursus
inque chori ludunt speciem lascivaque iactant   685
corpora et acceptum patulis mare naribus efflant.
de modo viginti (tot enim ratis illa ferebat)

restabam solus. pavidum gelidoque trementem
corpore vixque meo firmat deus "excute" dicens
"corde metum Diamque tene!" delatus in illam   690
accessi sacris Baccheaque sacra frequento.'
'praebuimus longis' Pentheus 'ambagibus aures,'
inquit 'ut ira mora vires absumere posset.
praecipitem, famuli, rapite hunc cruciataque diris
corpora tormentis Stygiae demittite nocti.'   695
protinus abstractus solidis Tyrrhenus Acoetes
clauditur in tectis; et dum crudelia iussae
instrumenta necis ferrumque ignesque parantur,
sponte sua patuisse fores lapsasque lacertis
sponte sua fama est nullo solvente catenas.   700

perstat Echionides, nec iam iubet ire, sed ipse
vadit, ubi electus facienda ad sacra Cithaeron
cantibus et clara bacchantum voce sonabat.
ut fremit acer equus, cum bellicus aere canoro
signa dedit tubicen pugnaeque assumit amorem,   705
Penthea sic ictus longis ululatibus aether
movit, et audito clamore recanduit ira.
monte fere medio est, cingentibus ultima silvis,
purus ab arboribus, spectabilis undique, campus:
hic oculis illum cernentem sacra profanis   710
prima videt, prima est insano concita cursu,
prima suum misso violavit Penthea thyrso
mater et 'o geminae' clamavit 'adeste sorores.
ille aper, in nostris errat qui maximus agris,
ille mihi feriendus aper.' ruit omnis in unum   715
turba furens; cunctae coeunt trepidumque sequuntur,
iam trepidum, iam verba minus violenta loquentem,
iam se damnantem, iam se peccasse fatentem.
saucius ille tamen 'fer opem, matertera' dixit
'Autonoe! moveant animos Actaeonis umbrae.'   720
illa quis Actaeon nescit dextramque precantis
abstulit, Inoo lacerata est altera raptu.
non habet infelix quae matri bracchia tendat,

trunca sed ostendens deiectis vulnera membris
'aspice, mater!' ait. visis ululavit Agaue 725
collaque iactavit movitque per aera crinem
avulsumque caput digitis complexa cruentis
clamat: 'io comites, opus hoc victoria nostra est.'
non citius frondes autumni frigore tactas
iamque male haerentes alta rapit arbore ventus, 730
quam sunt membra viri manibus direpta nefandis.
talibus exemplis monitae nova sacra frequentant
turaque dant sanctasque colunt Ismenides aras.

Commentary

511–81 Pentheus

Pentheus was the king of Thebes who rejected the introduction of the worship of Bacchus and who was punished by the god for his impiety.

511–12 *cognita res* literally means 'thing discovered' but here means more 'the discovery of the matter'. The seer referred to as *vati... auguris* is Tiresias who had prophesied the fate of Narcissus (348). Ovid makes the same point in different words in these lines – the spreading of the prophet's fame being equivalent to his having 'great renown' (literally 'name').

513 *Echionides* means 'son of Echion' and refers to Pentheus. The use of the 'patronymic' is common in epic poetry (cf. how Aeneas is called *Anchisiades* in Virgil's *Aeneid*), but has more point here as it reminds us of the ancestry of the king from the 'sown men', one of whom was his father Echion. These 'sown men' (*spartoi*) were the men who emerged from the ground after the sowing of the dragon's teeth: Echion was one of few left alive after the sown men had finished their civil strife, and so Pentheus' ancestry is both blood-stained and inhuman.

513–16 The contrast between the fame and respect shown to Tiresias by everyone else and the violent contempt felt for him by Pentheus alone (*ex omnibus unus* ('he alone out of everybody')) is well brought out here by the three strong verbs: *spernit* ('rejects') starts the sentence balanced and echoed by *ridet* ('laughs at') at the end of line 514 and concluded with the third verb *obicit* ('throws it in his face') emphasised by its position at the end of the sentence and the beginning of line 516. Pentheus is described as a 'despiser of gods' just as Mezentius in Virgil *Aeneid* 7.648 is called *contemptor divum*, and the signposting of this impiety is a powerful signal that all will end badly for him in the light of the previous stories in this book of gods avenging slights to their honour.

515 *tenebras et cladem lucis ademptae* is again something of a repetition: the 'darkness' is the blindness which is referred to as 'the disaster of his lost sight', with the word 'light' (*lucis*) substituted for 'sight' in metonymy. The language is expressive, as the 'darkness' of *tenebras* is well contrasted with the 'light' of *lucis* and the term *cladem* ('disaster') is ironically portentous as it is Pentheus who will suffer the 'disaster' in what is to come.

516 We know from the previous line (*senis*) that Tiresias is old; Ovid brings out the visual picture with the phrasing *albentia tempora canis* ('temples white with grey hair') and the dramatic head-shaking in *movens*.

517–18 Tiresias sees the future and so can foretell what is in the best interest of others even when they seem to be in control. Here he turns Pentheus' mockery of his blindness around by stating that Pentheus too (*tu quoque*) would be better off blind as then he would not see the Bacchic rituals. The imperfect subjunctives here are unreal conditionals in present time ('how happy you would be (now), if you were (already) blind...'). There is interesting variation of vocabulary here as *lucis ademptae* in lines 515 becomes *luminis orbus* in line 517. Tiresias' words are all the more powerful for the spitting sibilant alliteration of *felix esses si...luminis huius* and also for the heavy spondees which impart weight and power to the sentiments.

518 In Euripides' play *Bacchae* Pentheus is lured by Dionysus (Bacchus) onto the hillside to spy on the women performing his rituals and is there spotted by them and murdered by his mother and her sisters.

519 *auguror* picks up *auguris* in line 512. *procul* often means 'far off' in spatial terms; here it denotes far off in time.

520 *veniat* is present subjunctive and is most probably in a relative final clause ('the day on which the new Liber is to come').

The Greek god Dionysus was also known as *Lyaeus* ('the loosener' or 'liberator') and this is matched by the Roman use of the name *Liber* (which literally means 'free' and was the name of an Italian god of vegetation) for Bacchus, the Roman equivalent of Dionysus. The god was born of the union of the god Jupiter/Zeus and the mortal woman Semele who was tricked by Jupiter's jealous wife Juno into asking her divine lover to use the full power of his divinity in their lovemaking and who was destroyed in the ensuing conflagration. The child Bacchus was rescued from the dying woman and implanted in the thigh of Jupiter from where he was 'born' later on. The story has been told by Ovid earlier in this book at lines 253–315.

521 *fueris dignatus* is the 'periphrastic' future perfect equivalent to *dignatus eris* ('you will have thought him worthy'). Latin regularly uses the future perfect tense for the 'protasis' ('if…') section and then the future indicative (as here *spargere…foedabis*) in the 'apodosis' ('then…') section. *dignor* has the root sense 'think it right' but here it has the strong sense of *dignus* and so the whole sentence: 'if you do not think him (i.e., Liber) worth honouring with temples, then you will be scattered, torn to pieces, in a thousand places…' *templorum* is a defining genitive ('honour consisting of temples').

522 the violence is well brought out by the juxtaposition of *lacer spargere* and also by the exaggeration of *mille*, as well as the visual imagery of the blood (*sanguine*) and the alliteration of *l* in *mille lacer ... locis* and *s* in *sanguine silvas*. The prophet's words will come all too true, as line 722 *lacerata est* picks up *lacer* here. *spargere* is equivalent to *spargeris* (second person singular future passive: 'you will be scattered').

523 Pentheus' mother was called Agaue and her two sisters named in the incident are Ino and Autonoe. The prophecy shows us the location of the event before zooming in on the human agents involved and affected by the horrible business, with the spondaic word *foedabis* powerfully placed in enjambement showing the 'foulness' of the deed.

524 Tiresias turns from conditional sentences to firm statement of the future with strong indicative verbs: *eveniet, dignabere, quereris*. The prophet both recalls his own earlier words (*dignatus honore* (521) – *dignabere. honore* (524)) and also the king's mockery of his blindness (*tenebras* (515) – *tenebris* (525)) with the tart paradox that the king will lament that the old man saw too much in his darkness.

526 *Echione natus* ('son of Echion', literally 'born from Echion') recalls *Echionides* in 513 and forms a neat closural device for this paragraph. The strong verb *proturbat* in a vivid historic present tense suggests that the king roughly handles the old man and the present participle shows that the prophet was still speaking when he was shoved away.

527 Time has moved on and the prophet's words came true: the present participle *dicentem* is picked up in the perfect passive participle *dicta*. The word *fides* means here 'the fulfilment of a wish/ prayer' and so here means simply that his words came true. The poet again stresses the veracity of the words by repeating the sentiment in different words: 'and the prophet's responses are fulfilled'.

528 No sooner said than done, Liber is present in a short quick sentence showing the speed of his appearance, followed at once by the full clamour of his worship. The instantaneous spread of the ritual is shown by the rapid sequence of this line where the noise breaks out as soon as the god's presence is announced. The line is heavily onomatopoeic: the alliteration of *f* and the howling vowels of *ululatibus* are highly effective, as is the metaphor of the fields roaring with the cries.

529–30 Ovid well brings out the general melée in these lines to show that the worship of Bacchus was performed by both sexes and all classes, even though these were rites they were not familiar with (*ignota*). The confusion of gender and age is well brought out by the rapid catalogue of *mixtaeque viris matresque nurusque* (men, mothers, younger women (literally 'daughters-in-law')) and the social mixing is neatly emphasised by the juxtaposition of *vulgusque proceresque* (the common folk and the leaders), all joined with a long string of connecting uses of *que*. The rapidity of the movement and its confusion is enhanced by the signposting of *turba* at the start of the sentence, the short swift present tense *ruit* followed at once by *mixtae*. The Roman state had also been very uneasy when the Bacchanalia began to admit men to what had been an exclusively female cult (see Introduction and Livy 39.15.9–14).

531–63 Pentheus' speech

This speech attempts to appeal to the Thebans' feelings of patriotic pride and also their sense of shame. They have achieved so much and yet here seem unable to stand up to a pathetic effeminate enemy. The speech makes use of standard rhetorical features – the indignant rhetorical questions (531–42 is a series of four such, and the speech

draws to a conclusion with the indignant question about Acrisius in
559–61), the tricolon crescendo (534–5), the direct address to sections
of the audience (538, 541), the striking contrast between the formi-
dable enemy the snake and this bunch of women, as well as the obvious
uses of metre, alliteration and assonance which the commentary will
pick up. The arguments Pentheus uses are not so much the usual
pre-battle sentiments of 'liberate your country and die if need be' (such
as we find in e.g. Aeschylus *Persai* 401–5) but closer to the contemp-
tuous language of Menelaus addressing his own men in Homer's *Iliad*
7.96–102 ('Greek women, not Greek men any longer') or the dismissive
reassurance of a Gylippus at Syracuse in Thucydides 7.66–8, seeking
to inspire his men to face what he saw as a disorganised and shoddy
bunch of Athenians. Pentheus takes victory for granted and so sees
Theban failure to engage as a failure of courage and mettle, contrasting
the new enemy unfavourably with the real foes they faced in the past.

The argument can be summarised thus:

(a) You must be mad to let this bunch of wine-crazed women
     defeat you (531–7)
     - you old men made the heroic journey here only to be
       defeated thus (538–40)
     - you younger men should be girt with weapons rather than
       the thyrsus. Remember your ancestors and take on the spirit
       of the dragon which defeated some brave men – whereas you
       are facing effeminates. (540–7)
(b) If Thebes is fated to fall let it be at the hands of men not
     women, leaving us with defeat without shame. (548–52)
(c) This enemy is a boy and I will have him arrested; Acrisius stood
     up to Bacchus – and so will I.

531 The Thebans are called 'dragon-born' because their founding
ancestor Cadmus peopled his new city of Thebes with men born

from the teeth of the dragon whom he had killed; Cadmus had also married Harmonia, the daughter of Mars and Venus and so Thebans claimed descent from Mars (as did Ovid's Roman audience whose own foundation myth involved twins (Romulus and Remus) born of the god Mars and a priestess). The appeal to be true to one's forebears was a common theme of ancient oratory and epic poetry, and here the sense is that people born of such strong ancestors should not behave in this insane manner.

532–7 Pentheus mocks the Bacchic cult by reducing it to its component parts. His long sentence is beautifully constructed, with the tinkling cymbals of the Bacchic 'bronze clashing against bronze' contrasted with the real *bellicus ensis* (the insignificance of the former being hinted at in the ironical use of *tantum* which means 'so much'), the 'pipe with a curved horn' contrasted unfavourably with the truly fearful trumpet (alliteration of *t* bringing out the sound of the *tuba terruerit*), 'magic tricks' against the 'ranks of troops with their weapons drawn'. Pentheus makes effective use of the tricolon crescendo with repetition of *non* in 534–5 to build up the formidable foe of the past only to contrast this with the current enemy, described with hatred and contempt for what he sees: womanly voices (even though we know there are men there they are *behaving* like women), madness brought on by wine (apt for Bacchus who was the god of wine amongst other things but here discrediting the whole exercise), filthy animals (*grex* denoting a group of animals and thus suggesting that here people are behaving like animals in all their shameless sexuality) and drums which are *inania* – literally 'empty' as they must be to sound at all but which here suggests their futility and pointlessness. The speech thus conveys Pentheus' view that the rites are both silly and also licentious, disgraceful and the result of a fraud perpetrated by 'Bacchus', shameless especially for Thebans with their noble military valour.

538–40 Pentheus singles out the old men first for criticism and reminds them that they shared Cadmus' perilous voyage from Tyre in Phoenicia to found Thebes. This would make the old men the same generation as Pentheus' grandfather Cadmus (father of the king's mother Agaue). The subjunctive *mirer* in the question form is a deliberative or rhetorical subjunctive ('am I to admire you?'). The language is an effective rebuke: the old men made a long sea journey (*longa per aequora vecti*, wording reminiscent of Catullus 101) and pitched Tyre in this place (*Tyron* being accusative case), giving their fugitive household gods a place to rest here rather as the fugitive Trojans were told to bring their household gods to Italy in Virgil's *Aeneid* 2.293, only to be 'captured' without a fight now. *penates* are gods of the household, a very Roman institution and anachronistic in this Theban context. The contempt is enhanced by Pentheus' spitting *p* alliteration of *profugos posuistis...penates* as well as by the rhetorical repetition of *hac...hac* and most of all by the way in which he describes the men's past achievements in lengthy glowing clauses (lines 538–9) only to dismiss their current (*nunc*) madness in five short words (*nunc...capi*). *Marte* is ironic: it is metonymic for 'warfare' and so means 'without a fight' but it recalls the mention of Thebans' ancestry alluded to in line 531.

540–2 Pentheus now turns to the younger men, asking the same question (*mirer* understood as repeated from line 538) and asserts his connection with them as being closer to him in age (*propior meae (aetati)*). He addresses them as *acrior aetas* ('a more fierce age-group') and his use of *o* shows his high emotion here. Once again he uses neat parallels to show the gap between what they should be (*decebat*) doing and the reality of what they are in fact doing: they should have *arma* rather than *thyrsos*, they should be protected by a *galea* rather than a feeble *fronde*. The *thyrsus* was a ritual staff wreathed in ivy and vine-leaves and used by Bacchants: Pentheus is wrong to dismiss it as a forceful implement – Euripides tells us that it can injure (*Bacchae* 762–3) and can also work miracles, making water spring from a rock (704–5) and Horace (*Odes* 2.19.8) describes Bacchus as *gravi metuende thyrso* ('one to be feared for his powerful thyrsus'). The *fronde* referred to was the ivy which was worn by Bacchants to commemorate the use of these leaves by the nymphs of Mount Nysa to protect the infant Bacchus from the anger of his father's jealous wife Juno.

543 Pentheus appeals to their ancestry; 'remember from what stock you have been formed'. The Thebans were descended from the *Spartoi* who sprang from the dragon's teeth (see 531n. above). The dignity of the sentiment is enhanced by the spondaic phrase *qua sitis stirpe* and also by the sibilant alliteration.

544–5 'Be like the dragon who killed many people' may sound strange as the dragon was the beast who might have killed their founder Cadmus, but Ovid builds this up in the following lines in a series of contrasts between the young men's collective feebleness and the dragon's sole strength on the one hand and then between the animal needs of the one and the virtuous valour of the men. *animos* is plural, but this need not be pressed too hard: the men are to have 'spirits' such as that of the dragon, and the dragon had his 'tempers' as he killed people. As events turn out, Pentheus will be the one killed, and the phrase used there (715: *ruit omnis in unum*) is an ironic reversal – not 'one against many' but rather 'all against one'.

545 The dragon was merely defending his watery abodes: the Thebans now need to defend their reputation. *pro* means 'fighting for' as in *pro patria* ('for the fatherland') to be found on war memorials. Pentheus brings out the contrast by his use of the pronouns *ille* and *vos* in this and the following lines.

546 The line begins with the emphatic *interiit* followed by a pause: it then has a strong imperative in the fifth foot (*vincite*) as does the following line (*pellite*). The final syllable of *interiit* is long in this case (as if it were a contraction of *interivit*).

547 The contrast here is between the 'brave' men killed by the dragon and the 'effeminates' whom the young men need to drive out. The adjective *mollis* means 'soft' and is usually applied to women or to effeminate men. The word is grammatically ambiguous but here has to be accusative to give an object to the imperative *pellite*, as well as balancing *fortes*. For the rhetoric of 'womanly men' cf. Menelaus in Homer *Iliad* 7.96 ('you Greek women, no longer men') – an insult already bandied at them by Thersites in *Iliad* 2.235.

548 'Hold on to the glory of your ancestors' is a common appeal before a battle, whose intention is to preserve the status quo.

548–50 If Thebes were destined to fall, then let it fall at the hands of men rather than women, so that shame is not added to their defeat. Again, a familiar argument from e.g. Sophocles *Antigone* 679–80. The language of the sentence is strained: what starts out looking like a conditional (*si fata vetabant*) where the indicative suggests that *si* means 'even if (as a matter of fact) fate was (all along) forbidding...': only to switch to a wish clause for the present (*utinam* + imperfect subjunctive) – 'would that it were siege engines and men who were destroying the walls'. Pentheus uses the masculine language of warfare to stir up his audience: *tormenta virique/ moenia...ferrumque ignisque*. 'Fire and sword' is a common enough combination in rhetoric (cf. Cicero *Philippic* 11.37, *In Catilinam* 3.1, Livy 5.14.7) and is made more effective here by the use of auditory imagery in the verb *sonarent* ('would resound'), as in Virgil *Aeneid* 2.705–6.

551-2 Pentheus expresses the sentiment in three different ways: (a) we would not face any charge (of cowardice), (b) we could openly lament our fate and not hide it (in shame), and (c) our tears would not be ones tinged with shame. All three are the second half of the conditional implicit in the previous sentence – 'if it were men who were destroying the walls, then...' Pentheus brings out the suffering of defeat (*miseri...querenda...lacrimae*) to emphasise the attendant shame (*crimine...celanda...pudore*) which in this case would make the suffering a disgrace as well as a defeat. *foret* is the alternative form of *esset* (imperfect subjunctive of *sum*). Ovid makes the points in different words – *essemus sine* is similar to *carerent*, as *crimine* corresponds to *pudore*. *sors* ('destiny') picks up *fata* from line 548.

553-6 After the unreal subjunctives of lines 549–52 with their alternative world where defeat could be seen as noble, Pentheus brings his audience to the reality facing them now (*at nunc*) with a strong future indicative verb (*capientur*) and a derisory snort of indignation for the enemy they are facing – a boy (*puero*), who is not even armed (*inermi* postponed for effect to the end of the line) who does not even *like* fighting but rather enjoys dressing up as a woman. For the contemptuous use of *puer* cf. Mark Antony's famous jibe at the young Octavian: *tu puer, qui omnia nomini debes* ('you boy who owe everything to your name', quoted Cicero *Philippic* 13.11).

554-6 The tastes of Bacchus are conveyed in two groups: the three things he does not like (*bella...tela...usus equorum*, all three the subjects of *iuvant*) followed by the more expressively described group of four things he does enjoy (*madidus...crinis*; *mollesque coronae*; *purpura*; *pictis...aurum*), which are also the subjects of *iuvant*.

555 For the contempt for perfumed hair, especially associated with men from the East, cf. Turnus' prayer to the gods to let him 'befoul in the dust his (Aeneas') hair, curled as it is with hot iron and soaked with myrrh (*murraque madentes*)' (Virgil *Aeneid* 12.99–100; a sentiment also expressed by the African Iarbas in *Aeneid* 4.215–17). Myrrh is a a fragrant substance produced from the gum of the myrrh-tree. Bacchus came from the East as he explains in the prologue to Euripides' *Bacchae* (lines 1–63). *crinis* is singular here standing for the plural 'hair'; *madidus* also means 'drunk' and here adds a further implied slur to his character, as the *m* alliteration supports. Garlands (*coronae*) were worn as the symbols of military victory but were also worn at drinking-parties: here they are the 'effeminate' (*molles*) party-gear rather than anything manly, but the 'victorious' sense is also there in the suggestion that this softie is going to defeat them in battle.

556 *purpura* is the exotic and hugely expensive cloth stained with the dye taken from the *murex* shellfish and proverbially costly and decadent. Bacchus completes his outfit with 'gold woven into his decorated clothes', with the interlacing word order perhaps reflecting the interweaving of the colours alluded to: Ovid leaves open whether it is the gold which is the decoration of his clothes or whether they are already decorated with other colours and gold is added as a finishing touch. Gold is of course obviously expensive but it is also a soft metal whose presence in the clothing would add colour but no protection to this unarmed (*inermi*; line 553) boy.

557 *actutum* is a very rare archaic word meaning 'at once' and the line reads as a reminiscence of an earlier poet such as Pacuvius (220–130 BC) who composed his own account of this story in a now lost play entitled *Pentheus*. The elisions in *quid(em) eg(o) actutum* are themselves archaic and the word *actutum* occurs only once in Virgil and only here in Ovid. This, and the parenthetic use of *modo vos absistite* all make the line more dramatic and effective. The confident

final word of the line *cogam* ('I will force him') is rash and soon to be proved false.

558 Bacchus claimed that his father was Jupiter, but Pentheus does not believe this and promises to compel Bacchus to admit his 'falsely claimed' (*assumptum*) father and his 'invented rites' (*commenta* comes from *comminiscor*), with *esse* implied going with both terms. Bacchus will prove his true divinity by exacting punishment on the impious king (cf. Euripides *Bacchae* 47: 'I will prove that I am a god').

559 Acrisius also denied that Bacchus was a god and ended up regretting this when the women of Argos were driven mad by the god, although he was more famous for his attempt to defy destiny by imprisoning his daughter Danae in a tower to stop her producing the child who was destined to kill him (see Sophocles *Antigone* 944–54). Acrisius did not therefore die at the hands of Bacchus, and so although he ceases his resistance to the god later, he is a role-model here for Pentheus, whose death will prevent him from seeing Acrisius' change of heart.

559–61 Pentheus contrasts himself unfavourably and indignantly with Acrisius: 'does Acrisius have enough spirit (*satis animi*) to despise his empty godhead and lock the gates of Argos in his face (*venienti* is dative of disadvantage: "to him as he came"), but the stranger will terrify Pentheus and the whole of Thebes?' There is effective juxtaposition here of *contemnere vanum* (to despise it as being empty) and note also the repeated infinitives in fifth-foot position (*contemnere, claudere*). Pentheus names himself haughtily in 561, his name balanced by the name of his city at the end of the line, and his alliteration of t suggests his indignation; as does his lack of any connective between the sentence *an satis...portas* and the next line, where we expect a 'however'.

562 *citi* here means 'quickly' and is adverbial in sense. Notice the repeated *ite* showing his impatience. *ducem* refers to Bacchus who is 'leading' the people of Thebes into the confusion described at lines 529–30.

563 A slightly odd phrase, literally meaning: 'let sluggish delay stay away from my orders'. The adjective *segnis* is unnecessary but adds force to *mora*.

564–5 The chorus of opposition to Pentheus is well brought out in the tricolon crescendo of 564, with three increasingly long phrases all beginning *hunc*: *hunc avus – hunc Athamas – hunc cetera turba suorum/ corripiunt.* The *avus* is Cadmus himself, while Athamas was the husband of Ino, the sister of Pentheus' mother Agaue. The rest of 'his folk' (*suorum*) are summed up as a *turba* (cf. 529).

565 *corripiunt* here means 'rebuke' or 'censure' and the verb is strengthened by its position in enjambement at the start of the line. *frustra...laborant* go neatly together: for all their efforts (*laborant*) their words are 'in vain'.

566 *admonitu* is a causal ablative: he is made all the keener 'by their reproof'. The subject of *irritatur* is *rabies* in the next line. The metaphor is strong here: the 'rage' (*rabies*) is goaded by being held back (*retenta*) and grows (*crescit*), the suggestion being that the opposition made his eagerness all the greater and more inflamed, a device used in Ovid *Amores* 3.4.11.

567 The very (*ipsa*) means used to restrain him (*moderamina*) did more harm than good: literally 'they caused harm'. The verb *nocebant* is a summarising imperfect tense after the vivid present indicatives *est, irritatur, crescit.*

568–71 A good analogy to illustrate the poet's point, spoken in the first person with the authority of a didactic rather than an epic poet (*ego...vidi*: cf. for instance Lucretius 6.1044). The king's rage is increased by obstruction just as a stream is made to flow more violently by being dammed. This use of analogy is familiar from the similes in epic poetry (e.g. Homer *Iliad* 16.384–93, where the roar of the charging horses was like the thundering of torrential rain) and also from the analogies found in philosophy (e.g. Plato's image of the democratic state being like a ship where the crew all take turns on the rudder with disastrous results (*Republic* 488)) and didactic literature (e.g. Lucretius' image of the old man reluctant to die being like a diner who does not know that it is time to leave the feast (*DRN* 3.938)).

568 *eunti* is dative singular of the present participle of *eo* and refers to the torrent in its movement. *qua* here means 'where', so the whole phrase means 'where there was nothing obstructing its flow'. The rhythm of the line is powerfully spondaic, helping to convey the solid mass of the torrent.

569 *lenius* refers to the greater smoothness of the flow: *strepitu* indicates the noise it makes, the ablative being one of manner.

570 The obstructions in the channel are well evoked here by the use of language: there are two sorts of natural obstacles, wood (*trabes*) and rocks (*saxa*) and there is a piling up of 'restraining' verbs in the participle *obstructa* added to the main verb *tenebant*; also the build-up of consonants in *obstructaque saxa* well evokes the impediment to the stream.

571 *lenius* implied that the water flowed as a clear stream: *spumeus* shows us water as 'foaming' and is reinforced in *fervens* (literally 'boiling' and so 'bubbling up'). The comparative *lenius* is further answered in the comparative *saevior*. *Ab obice* means 'as a consequence of the blockage': *a(b)* often has this meaning of 'as a result of'.

572–3 The subject of the verb must be the servants whom Pentheus had sent off at line 562. They now return bloodied (*cruentati*) from their encounter. The order of words for translation is: *negarunt domino – quaerenti ubi Bacchus esset – (se) vidisse Bacchum*: 'to their master, when he asked them where Bacchus was, they replied that they had not seen Bacchus'. The word *esset* is imperfect subjunctive as part of the indirect question construction after *quaerenti*.

574 The servants bring in Acoetes, whose narrative will occupy lines 582–691. He is described as a 'companion and a servant of the rites' and his arrival parallels the scene in Pacuvius' play *Pentheus* where the poet apparently produced Acoetes as the Bacchic worshipper brought in for questioning; in Euripides' *Bacchae* the god himself is brought before the furious king who does not believe that he is divine at all. *tamen* here picks up the previous line: they did not even 'see' Bacchus but they have captured this man here (*hunc*).

575 *manibus…ligatis* is an ablative absolute construction but also indicates the state he was in – 'with his hands bound behind his back'.

576 At this stage the man is simply *quendam*: his identity will soon be revealed in great detail. The phrase *Tyrrhena gente* means 'of Etruscan origin': the tradition (Herodotus 1.94) was that the Etruscans derived from Lydian refugees and so the term here means 'Lydian' as is shown when Acoetes reveals that he was from Maeonia in Lydia (583), just as Dionysus tells Pentheus that he was from Lydia in Euripides *Bacchae* 464. The participle *secutum* agrees with *quendam* and governs *sacra dei*: this man was a follower of the rites of the god.

577 Before he speaks, Pentheus stares at the unnamed prisoner and the force of the gaze is brought out by the initial use of the present indicative *aspicit* followed by the detail of his eyes 'which anger had made terrifying'. *tremendos* is a gerundive – literally 'to be feared'.

578 The details of the *poena* are not spelled out here – in Euripides *Bacchae* (356–7) the king threatens death by stoning. *vix* often means 'with difficulty' as in the case of Silenus finding it hard to keep his seat on the donkey at *Ars Amatoria* 1.544: here it is the king's reluctance to put off the punishment of the man which makes it hard for him to ask him for his story – a hesitant reluctance which is perhaps brought out by the slow spondees of *et quamquam poenae*.

579 The two uses of the vocative case of the future participle (*periture...dature*: 'you who are going to perish...and provide.') at either end of the line and the intensive use of *o* are marks of the king's haughty and grandiose way of speaking. Note also the separation of *tua* from *morte* and the eloquent use of *documenta* (from *doceo* ('I teach')) and meaning here something like 'lessons', along with the emphatic position of *morte* at the start of the following line after the enjambement and followed by a solemn pause after the end of the king's words (*ait*).

580–1 Pentheus cannot simply ask: 'who are you?' but has to tell the man (notice the king's peremptory imperative *ede*) to give his name and that of his parents and his homeland. He then switches to an indirect question ('tell me why...'). *moris novi* is something of a contradiction in terms as *mos* usually refers to the established ancestral custom (often termed *mos maiorum* ('the customs of our ancestors')) and here we have a 'new' custom. The word *novus* often signified 'dangerously new-fangled' as in the phrase *res novae* for 'revolution' or 'sedition' and here the word has exactly this sense in terms of religious innovation.

582–691 Acoetes' tale: Bacchus and the sailors

582 Pentheus has eyes which are terrifying (577) and yet Acoetes is 'free of fear' and his tale is told in a leisurely way full of homely details of the man's childhood and his astronomical knowledge. The figure of Acoetes is interesting as he appeared in Pacuvius' play on this subject in exactly this role, although there is no evidence that he narrated the tale of the sailors and this is probably Ovid's own invention as a means of linking his two narratives together. The tale of Bacchus' being taken by sailors who then pay for their impiety had been told in the seventh of the *Homeric Hymns*.

583 Acoetes answers Pentheus varying the order of the questions: he gives his name and then his *patria* (Maeonia was in the kingdom of Lydia, in what is now Turkey) and finally his parentage. The low social standing of Acoetes is something of which he is far from ashamed, and the following lines are expressive of the romantic idea of primitivity which Romans often expressed. The term *plebe* is very Roman and would be anachronistic in this Theban context.

584–5 Acoetes' father had no lands to leave to his son; the subject of the main verb *reliquit* is *pater* in line 584 and the word order is deliberately confused in a device known as hyperbaton. The order for translation is: *pater non reliquit mihi arva quae duri iuvenci colerent lanigerosve greges* ('father left me no fields for tough bullocks to cultivate, nor wool-bearing flocks'). The subjunctive *colerent* expresses purpose in the sense of 'fields for bullocks to cultivate'. *armenta* signifies cattle as opposed to the 'wool-bearing flocks' of sheep; *lanigeros* is an effective compound adjective already used by Ennius, Accius and Lucretius but is here no mere idle epithet – the sheep would have been useful to provide Acoetes with wool if he had had any, just as the (non-existent) cattle could have tilled the (non-existent) fields.

586 The force of *et ipse* is that father was poor like Acoetes, the word *pauper* being stressed by its position at the start of the line and the sentence.

586-7 This is a spendid description of the skill of fishing: a matter of tricking (*decipere*) the fish with a line (*lino*), hooks (*hamis*) and rod (*calamo*) and then landing them (*ducere*) as they flail (*salientes*). There were other methods of catching fish (with nets, or spears) but this method suits the skilful father of Acoetes.

588 His skill was his income – a neat way of saying that he owed his living to his abilities as a fisherman. The word *ars* frames the line as being the only thing which father had to hand on to his son.

589-90 The object of *accipe* is postponed to the following line and the end of the sentence, and *quas* (literally 'which') here means something more like 'whatever'. *studium* signifies both enthusiasm and application, and *successor* is the legal term for one who succeeds to property through inheritance, as is the more obvious term *heres* ('heir'). The verb *reliquit* is repeated from 585.

590-1 Acoetes' wistful sadness is well brought out by the 'legacy' of his father – water. The position of *unum hoc* and the heavy spondees of 591, along with the emotional elision of *un(um) hoc poss(um) appellare* is moving, as is the ending of the sentence with the key word *paternum*.

592 Acoetes longed for variety in his fishing and was clearly impatient with being 'stuck always on the same rocks'; the arid toughness of the rocks symbolising his life.

593–4 The order for translation is: *addidici flectere regimen carinae dextra moderante* ('I also learned the knowledge of turning the steering of a ship with my guiding right hand'). The prefix *ad-* conveys the sense that he was 'extending' his knowledge as a fisherman, while the terms *regimen* and *moderante* both convey the idea of control.

594–5 Sailing the seas required knowledge of the stars and Acoetes demonstrates this now. The 'Goat Star' Capella was said to be Amalthea transported to the heavens after her death; as Amalthea had been born in Olenus, the star is called 'Olenian'. This star rises at the start of the rainy season in October and so is named here the 'rainy star' (*pluviale sidus*).

595 Taygetes is one of the Pleiades, while the Hyades are a group of five stars in Taurus whose name in Greek means 'the raining ones' and who marked the start and end of the rainy season. The original Hyades had been the nurses of Bacchus. Arctos is the Great Bear. All these stars denote rainy and stormy weather and showed Acoetes looking out for his own welfare and avoiding the storms which could have wrecked his ship and cost him his life; he did this himself (note the first-person verb *notavi*) and he did so from observation (*oculis*) and not from mere hearsay or books.

596 The theme of self-protection continues in Acoetes' learning of the 'abodes of the winds and the ports which were suitable for ships'. The winds were said to be enclosed in Aeolia, where their master Aeolus released them at intervals as described in Homer *Odyssey* 10.21–2, Virgil *Aeneid* 1.50–64; the meaning here is that Acoetes learned where the winds came from and where they were most likely to spring up and cause him trouble.

597 Acoetes was journeying to Delos and found himself by chance (*forte*) putting in to Chios ('the shores of the Chian land'). His purpose in going to Delos is not discussed but we get the impression that he is no longer a mere fisherman and that he is engaged in larger trade with his new skills of seafaring.

598 The two verbs *applicor* and *adducor* are both passive in form but 'middle' in sense, meaning 'I put in at' and 'I bring myself', the verb of motion with its prepositional prefix (*ad-*) letting the accusative *litora* stand without any preposition. His self-confidence is again stressed with the words *dextris...remis* here meaning something like 'skilful use of the oars' and showing his awareness that landing a ship could be a dangerous business if the sailor were not experienced.

599 Acoetes describes his disembarkation with vivid present tenses and lively vocabulary: the jump from the ship (*saltus*) into the shallows (the jump was 'light' (*levis*)) and the sailor then lets himself sink into (*immittor*) the wet sand (*udae harenae*).

600 Acoetes put into Chios for the night: for all his star-gazing skills, he still prefers not to sail in the darkness and he gets up as soon as it is light. The rosy glow of dawn (*rubescere*) recalls the 'rosy-fingered dawn' of Homer (e.g. *Odyssey* 2.1). Acoetes' impatience to get moving is conveyed by the paratactic series of simple verbs – *coeperat, exsurgo* – showing that once dawn 'had started' he gets up.

601–2 Acoetes has 20 men as his crew (see line 687) to whom he gives orders. He bids them bring fresh water (*latices recentes*) and shows them where to find it (*undas* here means the spring of fresh water rather than the 'waves' of the sea). The subjunctive *ducat* is one of purpose – the way which *was to* lead them.

603 While the others were fetching water, Acoetes himself (*ipse*) goes up to a high mound to gauge the wind. He needs to predict what

the wind will do later on and so uses the expressive verb *promittat* ('promises') to see if it will take him to Delos rather than blow him elsewhere.

604 The eagerness of Acoetes is well conveyed in the three strong verbs here (*prospicio, voco, repeto*), as well as by the complex hyperbaton whereby he looks from the high mound and gauges the wind while he is there.

605 'Here we are, look!'. Opheltes is one of 11 sailors whom Ovid names in this tale.

606 Take *utque putat* after *praedam*. Opheltes got some 'booty – as he thought…'

607 The description of the 'boy with young girl's appearance' is different from the *Homeric Hymn* which describes him as being 'like a young man' but helps to explain why the sailors thought he would be an easy prey, especially when they decide in the next line that he is sleepy and/or drunk. The paradoxical mixture of genders is well stressed by the juxtaposition of *virginea puerum*.

608 'Heavy with unmixed wine and sleep' helps to explain why the sailors were so confident of taking him but is ironically apt for the god of wine who has no need to fear any mortal foe. *titubare* is a good word to express his 'staggering' footsteps as he finds it hard (*vix*) to follow Opheltes.

609–10 Acoetes, like a good captain, is ahead of his men in intelligence and sees that this is no mere mortal. He assesses the boy's dress (*cultum*), appearance (*faciem*) and movement (*gradum*) and deduces that there was nothing which could be thought to be mortal about any of them, the subjunctive *posset* being potential ('could'). This is possibly hindsight on the part of the narrator, and Acoetes does not specify how he came to this correct conclusion.

611–12 Acoetes stresses that he told his sailors this important realisation at once with the spondaic phrase *et sensi et dixi*, emphasising his meaning with the sharp chiastic repetition (*numen... corpore...corpore numen*). The word *numen* derives from the word for 'nodding' and indicates the divine power which can change things simply by a nod of the head.

613 'Whoever you are' is a common enough phrase in prayers to gods when we do not know their name but are sure of their power. *faveas, adsis, des* are all second person singular subjunctives forming polite requests ('please would you...'). Humans seek the favour of the gods as their disfavour is often catastrophic, as has been shown in many stories in this poem already. *laboribus* indicates 'endeavours' as well as 'toils'.

614 'Forgive these men' – for they know not what they do, implies Acoetes here. The men immediately reply with a shrug: 'stop praying on our behalf'. *mitto* + infinitive is common with the sense 'give up (doing something)'.

615–16 The speaker was Dictys, who is now briefly described as a brilliant crew-member. The subtext of the lines is however that for all his swiftness as a sailor he was fatally slow as a judge of disguised gods. *quo* is ablative of comparison with *ocior* ('swifter than whom') and the sentence thus means: 'than whom no one was swifter at climbing the topmost yard-arms and sliding back down after grasping the rope'. The infinitive *ascendere* is 'epexegetic' (i.e. explanatory) with *ocior* ('swifter "at" climbing'), while *prenso rudente* is both ablative absolute ('the rope having been grasped') and also instrumental (he slid down using the grasped rope).

617–19 Epic poetry likes lists and catalogues, going back to Homer's 'catalogue of ships' in *Iliad* 2, recalled in the gathering of Italian forces in Virgil *Aeneid* 7. Earlier in this book (206–25) we had the wonderful catalogue of Actaeon's dogs. Here Ovid gives us a brief list of the crew members who gave their approval, linked by the anaphora of *hoc… hoc*. The purpose of this brief list is to give the detail which makes Acoetes' tale more authoritative, and also to excuse his inability to stand against so many opponents in his view of Bacchus.

617 Melanthus' job was to be forward lookout, and there is a nice irony in the fact that Melanthus (whose name in Greek means 'black flower') has fair hair (*flavus*).

618–19 Alcimedon has another significant name: in Greek this would mean 'strong ruler' and the name stresses the force of his opposition. Epopeus (whose name in Greek means 'watcher-out') was what we might call the cox: he used his voice to give the rhythm (*modum*) and the intervals between the strokes (here termed 'rest' (*requiem*) rather as a break between musical notes is termed a 'rest'). The regular pattern of: rest – stroke – rest – stroke etc. is well brought out by the repeated -*que* in *requiemque modumque*. Acoetes nicely has the rhythm and the rest being given to the oars (*remis*) rather than the oarsmen themselves (although obviously it is the latter who are meant) and is the 'encourager of their spirits', *hortator* being the term used in this context for the cox.

620 Rather than name all the other crew, Acoetes summarises by telling us that the others all felt the same, the verb to be understood being *probant*. The moral point is then drawn by the statement of

their base motive: 'so blind was their lust for booty', and the use of assonance of *ae* and alliteration of *c*, *p*, and *d* helps to underline this key point. Blindness is a theme which is developed throughout book 3, from Tiresias' all-seeing blindness to the blindness of the servants who did not see Bacchus (573) to the blindness of Pentheus' mother as she murders her own son.

621–2 Acoetes stands on his authority and stands up to the crowd. 'No matter (*tamen*) – I will not allow this pinewood ship to be defiled with its holy cargo – I have the greatest authority in this matter'. *pinum* literally means 'pine tree' and is a good use of synecdoche as the material which made the ship is used to stand for the ship itself; and Acoetes' authority is shown in his confident use of the future indicative *perpetiar*. The phrasing of *sacro violari pondere* is deliberately shocking: what he means is that he will not allow them to kidnap this god and so violate the ship by acting in an impious manner, but he expresses this with the paradox that the 'sacred weight' will 'pollute' the ship.

623 The verbs are in the vivid present tense as Acoetes tells his exciting story and the clash of the two men is well brought out by the juxtaposition of *obsisto. furit*. The *aditus* was the 'way in' for the ship and so would be something like a 'gangplank'. *furit* is a good word to use here: it conveys both the rage felt at the captain's obstruction and also has a sense of 'madness' which is what their behaviour towards the god amounts to.

624–5 Lycabas had 'form' for violence: he had been expelled from his Lydian home for murder and was sailing the seas in exile. *exilium* and *poenam* are in apposition to each other – the punishment consisted in the exile. *Tuscus* means 'Etruscan' but here means 'Lydian' as the ancients believed that Etruria was colonised from Lydia (see 576n.). Ominously he is going to suffer even more in the next few lines.

626–7 Lycabas assaults Acoetes as he 'stands his ground' (*resto* means *resisto*): he 'shattered my throat with his young fist'. The adjective *iuvenali* suggests that Lycabas was younger and stronger than Acoetes and had the strength and the impetuosity of youth; the violence is brought out by the *u* assonance of *guttura pugno* and by the enjambement as the verb *rupit* is highlighted at the end of the phrase but the start of the next line.

627–8 Lycabas 'would have sent [Acoetes] hurled into the sea'; the sentence is a remote conditional in past time, explaining how it was that Acoetes managed to stay on board. *excussum misisset* has a lot of powerful sibilant alliteration (expressive of the anger involved) and is a good example of the juxtaposition of strong verbs: *excutio* is the word commonly used for throwing overboard, and ending the line with two monosyllables *si non* makes the narrator sound out of breath as he no doubt was after the punch. *amens* is formed from the 'alpha-privative' (or negating 'a') added to the word *mens* ('mind') and so means 'out of one's mind', 'stunned'. The point of the word here is that Acoetes grasped the rope (*fune*) without even thinking about it, his salvation being shown in the two words at either end of the line (*haesissem...retentus*).

630 Acoetes had been right all along of course – 'for it had been Bacchus' – and now Bacchus stirs and speaks. Earlier on (608) Acoetes had described Bacchus as behaving like one who is drunk or sleepy; he now returns to this theme, but *veluti* followed by the subjunctive *solutus sit* shows that he was not in fact asleep or drunk but only behaving as if he were awakened by the shouting, the drowsiness well conveyed by the *s* alliteration of *solutus/ sit sopor*.

631 *aque* is in fact *a + que* ('and from'); attaching *que* to a single-syllable preposition is unusual. The sense-organs are of course largely

in the head, but the ancients commonly believed that the seat of understanding and thought is in fact in the breast rather than the brain (e.g. Lucretius *DRN* 3.140).

632–3 Bacchus fires four questions at the men, each beginning with a different question word, and developing in sophistication (almost as if he really were just waking up) from basic 'what are you doing?' and 'what [is this] shouting?' to 'by what means, sailors, have I arrived here?' and 'where are you preparing to take me?' *ops* means literally 'power' or 'ability' and the question *qua ope* suggests that Bacchus is aware that they seem to have overcome a god – for the moment. The tone of the questions suggests that Bacchus is in their hands ('where are you taking me?') whereas in fact of course they are soon going to be in his hands.

634–5 Proreus is the Greek word for the bow-man or forward lookout – the role of Melanthus (*prorae tutela*; 617). He now speaks patronisingly to Bacchus and promises to take him wherever he would like to go. This is obviously a lie – sailors have their voyages planned with a destination in advance and would not be able to make any detour to suit a stranger on board. It insults the intelligence of the god and will not do the crew any favours. The order of translation is: *ede quos portus velis contingere* ('tell us which ports you would like to reach'). *sistere* is the second person singular future passive of *sisto* and so is a strong statement – 'you will be landed' – while *petita* agrees adjectivally with *terra* ('on the desired land').

636–7 Naxos needs no preposition – like all small islands, towns and cities. *Naxon* is the Greek accusative ending of *Naxos*. Naxos was a centre of worship of the god Bacchus, having been seen by some as his birthplace and as the place where Bacchus rescued the princess Ariadne after Theseus had left her there. Bacchus offers the sailors hospitality in his *domus* there, like a good Roman or Greek host. The god produces a neat sentence here, with *mihi domus est* balanced by *vobis erit hospita tellus*.

638 *fallaces* agrees with the subject of the verb (the crew) and describes them as 'tricksters' or 'liars' who are willing to swear by the sea and all the gods when they know that they have no intention of doing as they promise. For sailors to perjure themselves by the sea is foolish in the extreme and is a mark of their madness here.

639 *fore* is the contracted future infinitive of *sum*: the sailors swear 'that it will be so'. The crew now order Aceotes to set sail – even though he is their master they have now taken charge of the vessel. The ship is *pictae* as many ancient ships were – painted with bands of colour and sometimes a pair of eyes. Acoetes tells a good story and fills it with this sort of vivid detail.

640 *dextra* here is ablative and means 'on the right' in both uses of the word in this line; *lintea do* means 'I direct the sails'. Acoetes is now steering the ship in the direction the god wants.

641–2 There is major textual problem here. If *pro se quisque* stands then it has to mean 'each man, shouting for himself, said...' and we have to imagine the crew shouting *quid facis...* in chorus. The manuscripts read *timet* and this has been emended to *tenet* to make better sense. *demens...furor* ('you madman!...what madness...') is ironic here as it is the crew who are mad rather than Acoetes.

642–3 Most of them gesture silently with a nod, others whisper into his ear (*aure* here means literally 'using my ear' but should be translated as if it were *in aurem*).

644 Acoetes' instant reaction is well brought out by a rapid dactylic line. *obstipui* is a strong verb: 'I was struck dumb'. Acoetes cannot resist the rest of the crew but he refuses to be the instrument of their folly and tells them to let somebody else take over the helm (*moderamina*). *aliquis* is purposefully vague – 'somebody' means 'anybody at all so long as it is not me'.

645 *sceleris artisque* is a hendiadys; 'I detached myself from being the servant of their crime and my skill' means that he refused to allow them to use his *ars* in pursuit of their *scelus*.

646 The unanimity of the condemnation of Acoetes is well brought out by the juxtaposition *cunctis totumque* and their incessant clamour is stressed by the repetition of similar ideas in the verbs *increpor... immurmurat*: the threatening force of their anger is also well conveyed in the heavy spondees of *a cunctis totumque imm-*.

647 *scilicet* ('I suppose') is heavily sarcastic here, as Aethalion takes over the helm stating that 'all our safety is placed in you alone', with the sibilant alliteration perhaps helping to show his scorn. The sarcasm is naturally misplaced irony, as subsequent events show and it turns out that their only hope of safety *was* to listen to Acoetes. The word order stresses the meaning: *omnis in uno* ('all...in one').

648–9 Aethalion's actions are swift and decisive: there are four verbs in the present tense in quick succession (*ait...subit...explet...petit*) and his contrary nature is highlighted by his steering towards the direction 'opposite to' (*diversa*) Naxos, leaving the supposed destination behind (*relicta* in the ablative agreeing with *Naxo* as an ablative absolute).

650 The whole sentence shows the god of the theatre at his playful best: Bacchus mocks (*illudens*) the sailors by feigning surprise and

helplessness, making himself look like (*similis*) one who was weeping (*flenti* is dative singular of the presente participle of *fleo*), 'as if' (*tamquam*) he had just noticed (*modo senserit*) at last their deceit. The irony is neat as the god responds to their deceit with deceit of his own.

651 There is effective *p* alliteration here as the 'boy' blubbers and stammers his feigned sadness.

652–5 Bacchus makes an impassioned short speech full of indignant questions, keeping up his role as the helpless victim. The balanced repetition of *non haec mihi litora...non haec mihi terra* in similar metrical positions in consecutive lines, the framing of line 653 with the parallel verbs *promisistis...rogata est*, then the double pairs of *quo...quae* and *si...si...*along with the oxymora of *puerum iuvenes* and *multi...unum* (arranged chiastically (A-B-B-A)) as he spells out the obvious unfairness of the situation. The main verb *promisistis* ('you promised') takes *non haec litora* as its object, while *non haec terra* is the subject of the passive verb *rogata est*. *quo* agrees with *facto* (literally 'by what deed?') and both *iuvenes* and *multi* are in agreement with the 'you' which is the subject of *fallitis*.

656 The narrator wept and his sorrow is stressed by the spondaic rhythm of *iamdudum flebam* as well as by the juxtaposition of *flebam: lacrimas*. Acoetes' tears are summarily mocked by the crew – *ridet* being stressed by its position in enjambement at the start of the line, when the 'unholy crew' (*manus impia*) laugh at him and sail quickly away, their haste well brought out by the phrasing *impellit aequora* ('[the crew] strikes the waves') *properantibus remis* ('with hurrying oars'), the interlaced word order itself suggesting the hurried motion of the oars.

658 The order for translation is: *adiuro nunc tibi per ipsum [deum]* ('I swear to you by the god himself'). *praesens* when used of a god means 'present and attentive to our prayers' and then also 'effective'. There is no god more *praesens* than that god (Bacchus).

659–60 Acoetes means that his words are as true as they seem to be untrue – a typical Ovidian paradox. *tam...quam* are correlatives ('so true...as they are...') used here with some concessive force ('I am telling a tale as true as it seems beyond belief'). The language is compressed: *veri fides* meaning 'faith in their truthfulness'. Acoetes forcefully repeats the pronoun *tibi* to the king and his alliteration of *t* (in *tam...tibi*) shows his excitement and certainty.

660–1 Bacchus now starts the transformation which makes this tale a fitting part of the *Metamorphoses*. The ship stood still on the waters just as if the 'dry shipyard' (*siccum navale*) held it fast, with the spondees of *siccum navale* suggestive of the static ship.

662 *admirantes* means 'in their amazed surprise' and the sluggish spondaic rhythm of the line (with every syllable heavy except for the expected dactylic fifth foot) well conveys their inability to move the static ship for all their efforts. *verbere* is used elsewhere of flogging people and here nicely depicts the men 'flogging' the oars against the water, their tenacity conveyed in *perstant*.

663 The oars are not working so they try to get the wind to move the ship by unfurling the sail. *deducunt* shows the men 'unfurling' the sail from the yardarm and the 'twin power' (*gemina ope*) is the use of oars and sails combined. *currere* is their wishful thinking: they will be lucky to move at all, let alone to 'run' especially when the ivy 'impedes' them in the next line.

664 The ship now disastrously begins to sprout the foliage appropriate to Bacchus. Ivy (*hederae*) clogs the oars and creeps up to the sails – and ivy was worn on the heads of worshippers of Bacchus. *impediunt* is stressed at the start of the line and the sentence, balanced and amplified by *serpunt* in the same position in the next line, its force being further enhanced by the enjambement. The entwining movement of the plant is well conveyed by the words *nexu recurvo serpunt* ('they creep with twisting coil') and the weight of the clusters (*gravidis corymbis*) helps to keep the ship still and prevent it moving. The verb *distinguunt* expresses the visual 'decoration' of the ship by the sudden growths.

666-7 *ipse* is Bacchus himself who now shows himself for what he is by *his* transformation from a boy into the god he was all along. *racemiferis* (formed from *racemus* + *fero* = 'cluster-bearing') is an impressive compound adjective, as grandiose as the god who now appears, and the god sports grapes (*uvis*) on his forehead. *circumdatus* (literally 'girdled') takes *frontem* as an accusative of respect ('wreathed as to his forehead'). The helpless boy is now armed with a spear, suitably wreathed with vine leaves as befits the god of wine, which he brandishes.

668-9 Bacchus is often seen accompanied by tigers and other wild animals, and this terrifying sight is well brought out here by the spondaic rhythm of the start of line 668, as Acoetes recalls this awesome part of his experience. Bacchus here has the retinue of tigers, lynxes and panthers but they are all unreal images (*simulacra inania* – the term which Lucretius (*DRN* 4.994-5) uses for dreams). They are convincing enough to terrify the sailors, but are just another aspect of the theatricality of this god and his ability to conjure images out of nowhere. The three sorts of animals are described in a tricolon crescendo, with tigers (one word) followed by lynxes (three words) and then the panthers given an entire line to themselves. The panthers are 'spotted' (*pictarum*) and again the word suggests the artificial nature of these images; the Greek word *pantherarum* unusually for Ovid takes up the whole of the final two feet of line 669, giving a fifth foot spondee and having a very 'Alexandrian' sound. The device is normally reserved for Greek loan words (as here), such as that in Cicero's spontaneous hexameter (*Letters to Atticus* 7.2.1):

flavit ab Epiro flavissimus Onchesmites

670 The men leapt up from the rowing benches, 'whether it was madness which made this happen or fear [I do not know]'. The verb switches to the perfect tense *exsiluere* denoting the rapid action completed in an instant, with the verb promoted to the first word of the line and the sentence and the dactylic rhythm of the line showing the rapid movement of the men.

671 The men now begin their metamorphosis into dolphins and Acoetes narrates the transformation with tremendous linguistic skill.

672 Medon began to grow dark 'in body' and to be bent (*flecti*) as the 'curve of his spine was forced out' – that is, as his back was forced up to curve sharply.

673 Lycabas 'begins [to speak] to this [man]' and describes his change as *miracula* (a thing to be wondered at, but here something like 'monster').

674 While he was speaking (*loquenti*) the nose was already rounded (*panda*) and the gaping jaws (*rictus*) broad (*lati*), with their owner in the possessive dative case (*loquenti* being the dative masculine singular of the present participle of *loquor*).

675 'The hardened skin took on scales' – an incorrect assertion, as
dolphins do not in fact have scales but have soft skin, but effective
for the hard consonants (*q, c, d, t*) in the Latin as the skin forms the
hard surface. The imperfect tenses of the verbs *erat* and *trahebat*
are striking: these events were happening while Acoetes was still
speaking (*loquenti*) and so the effect is of the events unfolding fright-
eningly almost in 'real time'.

676 Libys is trying to twist the oars out of the water, sliding the
oar-handles into the body of the ship and keeping the blades well
clear of the sea to stop them obstructing the natural floating of the
vessel, and the effort involved is well brought out by the spondees of
obstantes dum vult. 'But while Libys is trying (literally "wanting") to
ship the oars which are in the way'.

677 He saw his hands 'jump back' into a small compass, and now saw
that they were not hands any more but rather 'fins' (*pinnas*); Acoetes'
use of the verb *vidit* is especially striking as this takes us right into
the first-hand experience of Lycabas himself. Line 678 is wonderfully
balanced as Libys struggles to understand what has happened to him:
he first realises that they are not 'hands' any more and then sees that
they can be called fins, the repeated word *manus* showing his shocked
disbelief (cf. the repeated *bracchia* in lines 679–80).

679 After Medon, Lycabas and Libys we now have a nameless 'other
man' trying to work with arms which no longer exist. *dare bracchia*
indicates 'stretching out his arms', while the ropes he is stretching
towards are well described as *intortos* ('plaited' from *intorqueo* both
in the simple sense that rope is made from plaiting something such
as hemp, as well as the new plaits created by the ivy). Notice his
frustration and surprise when the arms in line 679 are not arms in
line 680.

680-1 After we have heard that he no longer had arms his body is described as *trunco* ('limbless', 'mutilated') and he leaps into the sea. *repandus* means 'flattened' and probably refers to the flattened face as Pacuvius had coined the compound adjective *repandirostrum* ('flattened beaked') to describe dolphins.

681 *novissima cauda* means 'the end of his tail'. A *falx* was a sickle and so *falcata* means 'sickle-shaped' or 'curved', although the simile in the next line suggests a broader curve than would be found in a sickle.

682 An effective and brief simile to compare the shape of the tail with the half-moon. *qualia* takes *cornua* and *dimidiae lunae* go together ('just as the horns of the half-moon').

683-4 The men now look like dolphins and they now also begin to behave like them. The 'leaping' (*saltus*) in 683 is presumably the remaining crew members leaping into the sea but the image elides nicely with the leaping of dolphins already in the water. *multaque aspergine rorant* ('they are drenched with much spray') as they sink and then they re-emerge (note the repetition of 'again and again' in *iterum redeuntque...rursus*, with *rursus* deriving originally from *reversus*). The gradual emerging from the water is evoked by the spondaic rhythm of *emergunt*, and the following dactyls suggest the rapid dancing above the waves.

685-6 *in chori...speciem* means 'looking like a dancing group'. The men were shocked to be transformed but they now show the happy playful behaviour always associated with dolphins: they 'play' (*ludunt*) and their bodies are 'frisky' (*lasciva*) as they 'toss them about' (*iactant*) and snort the sea water out of their spreading nostrils. *acceptum* can mean 'pleasing' as well as being the past participle of *accipio* (and so 'taken in'), which adds to the imagery of pleasure and joy in this passage.

687 *modo* – 'only a short time ago'. *de viginti* ('out of the twenty') shows the size of the original crew ('for that is how many that vessel was carrying').

688 The singular verb and the emphatic final word *solus* are eloquent in showing how only Acoetes survived the transformation intact.

688–9 Acoetes stresses the fear and cold: *pavidum gelidoque trementem* (agreeing with a *me* implied) where the 'trembling' is a result of the cold as well as the fear, and the cold is itself the paleness of shock; the phrase *corpore vixque meo* is wonderful: the body is 'scarcely my own' any more. The reassuring god however rewards his loyalty and gets his voyage to Naxos after all. There is a nice poignancy in the choice of *excute* for 'shake off (fear)' as this is the word used often of throwing people overboard (627).

690 *tene* here means 'make for' and is short for *cursum tene*. *delatus* must mean 'borne (by the winds)'.

691 Acoetes is now a firm devotee as is shown by the repeated *sacris...sacra*, the respectful naming of the god in adjectival form *Bacchea*, and the switch from the perfect *accessi* ('I joined') to the present continuous *frequento* ('I celebrate them assiduously'). We are not told how Acoetes made the journey from Naxos to Thebes; but it is clear that he now follows the rites of Bacchus wherever they go and so it is not implausible for him to come to Thebes to help set up what were 'unknown' (*ignota*; 530) rites at that time.

692–734 Pentheus' tale concluded

692 After the lively narrative, Pentheus responds with regal haughtiness, describing the detailed story as 'lengthy ramblings' (*longis*

ambagibus) and seeming to feel that he is owed gratitude for lending Acoetes his ears.

693 Pentheus' motive for listening is explained: so that the 'wrath could spend its strength by the passage of time'. This seems unlikely in view of Pentheus' next instructions.

694–5 The violence of these words suggests that his *ira* had lost none of its *vires. praeceps* usually means 'headlong, head-over-heels' and (after *rapite*) the image is of a man being hustled roughly and quickly forwards. *crucio* is to 'torment, torture' and the *tormentis* are unspecified instruments of torture: the 'Stygian night' is death; Styx was one of the rivers in the Underworld. The sequence of words is one of hideous cruelty: *praecipitem rapite...cruciataque diris...tormentis Stygiae demittite nocti* all conveying the wrath and the savagery of the king (*corpora* is plural for singular here), and the dactylic rhythm of line 694 well conveys the rapid fire of his cruel orders.

696 Acoetes is locked in prison awaiting his torture – a punishment which he of course does not deserve as he is defending the divinity of Bacchus. *abstractus* tells us that he was 'dragged away' and the prison is one that cannot be broken into or out of (*solidis*).

697–8 The 'cruel tools of the commanded execution, the iron and the fires, are being prepared'. The 'fire and sword' theme is Pentheus' typical way of acting as he stated in line 550.

699–700 'Of their own accord' (*sponte sua*) is stated twice at the start of the two consecutive lines and is not entirely accurate of course, as we know that the god is behind this rescue. This is how the story goes and the narrator even distances himself from the tale he is telling with the phrase *fama est* ('the story is told that...'), suggesting that this is what was told after the event. One almost pictures Acoetes cowering in his cell with eyes tightly shut. *nullo solvente* is ablative absolute with some concessive force ('although nobody untied them'), and we have to understand *esse* with *lapsas*.

701 Pentheus stands on his nobility of race, and the promotion of the spondaic verb *perstat* to the start of the line and the sentence well conveys his fixedness of purpose. He is called 'son of Echion' as he rises to the challenge of going in person (*ipse*) rather than sending anybody else to sort out the Bacchic rites.

702–3 'where Cithaeron – chosen for the celebration of the rites – resounded with the singing and the bright voices of the Bacchants'. Cithaeron was suitable for the rites as it was near Thebes, and it will be ideal for what is to come in the following lines. *Ad* + gerundive signifies purpose – this is why Cithaeron had been chosen. The assonance and alliteration of *Cithaeron/ cantibus et clara bacchantum voce sonabat* well convey the ringing sound and clear singing of the worshippers, a sound which inflames Pentheus' wrath further.

704–7 Ovid uses a brief epic simile comparing the effect of the Bacchants' singing on the king to the effect of a trumpet-blast on a fierce horse; both animal and king become all the more eager for the fight. The obvious point of comparison is the music and the effect on the savage beast/king, but there is also a clear ironic subtext as the horse is carrying an attacker whereas Pentheus will shortly by hunted down as victim by these singers. The simile is perhaps reminiscent of Homer's image of Paris going out to equally undistinguished fighting (*Iliad* 6.504–11) compared with a horse desperate to gallop out.

704 An expressive line, framed by words of sound (*fremit…canoro*) with *aere* (literally 'bronze') here standing for the bronze trumpet by

metonymy but also well placed next to *bellicus* as bronze has a warlike tone.

705 The *tubicen* is the man who makes the *tuba* 'sing' (*cano*). *amorem* may seem an odd word to use here, but is apt for the horse which 'takes on' the passion for fighting from the sound of the instrument.

706 Pentheus is the object of the verb *movit*, the subject being the *aether* which has been *ictus* by the lengthy 'howlings'. *ululatibus* is a very onomatopoeic word for the ritual noises, and *ictus* is foreshadowing the way in which Pentheus himself will shortly be 'struck' by more than music. The spondaic rhythm of *sic ictus longis* draws attention to this key moment in the story when his anger is rekindled by the noise, with the strong verb *movit* enhanced by its position in enjambement at the start of the next line.

707 There is a nice combination of verbs here showing the sequence of events: hearing (*audito*) causes the anger of the king to 're-glow', the repeated *c* sounds in *clamore recanduit* also showing the noise.

708 The death of Pentheus takes place halfway up a mountain. There is a clearing surrounded by woods but which itself is free of trees which might obscure the view either for Pentheus watching the Bacchants or for them seeing him. The line is taken up with two phrases in the ablative, the one being local ('on the middle point of a mountain') and the second being the absolute construction ('with woods encircling its edges'). The line neatly and economically sets the scene and the sense of being trapped (with the woods surrounding the hapless king) is ominous and apt.

709 *purus ab* means here 'free from', 'clear of' and also has the sense that this was in some ways a sacred and pure place, soon to be

defiled by the unholy presence of Pentheus with his *oculis profanis*. *spectabilis* means 'able to be overlooked' and also 'worth looking at' – strengthened by *undique* ('on all sides') – and helps to explain how this all came about: the topography helps Pentheus to see the women but it also means that they can see him, and he was something they were glad to see.

710–11 The sense is: *hic mater prima videt illum oculis profanis cernentem sacra* – 'at this the mother was the first to see him seeing the rites with his uninitiated eyes'. Note the sharp oxymoron of *sacra profanis* and the neat irony of the mother seeing Pentheus seeing the rites in which she was taking part. The word profanus means originally 'in front of the sanctuary' (*pro* + *fanum*) and so comes to mean 'uninitiated' and gives us our word 'profane'.

711–13 The tricolon crescendo of *prima...prima...PRIMA* is very effective, especially as it builds up the tension; we do not know who is meant by the adjective until line 713, when Agaue is described simply as 'mother' and the word *mater* given the greatest possible emphasis by being placed at the end of the sentence but at the start of a line. Euripides in the *Bacchae* (line 1114) also has the lead role in the murder of her son being taken by his mother Agaue who has been put into a hallucinatory trance by Dionysus/Bacchus.

711 *insano concita cursu* – 'whipped up in a mad charge': the alliteration adds to the violence of the attack about to happen and the word *insano* helps to emphasise the madness of the women, as does the striking phrase *turba furens* in line 716.

712 *violavit* is effective here, meaning to 'abuse, violate, disfigure'; note also *thyrso* which is the word used throughout Euripides *Bacchae* for the Bacchic wand, sneered at by Pentheus at 542 but here

used as a missile against him. The possessive adjective *suum* is highly pointed here as it was 'her own' son whom she killed, and the case is made more poignant still by Pentheus being named. The woman assaulted 'her own Pentheus', the name which she called him (when she was in her right mind) being added for pathetic effect.

713 The vocative *o* is generally used in states of high emotion (Lucretius 2.14) or in cases of religious ritual as here and at Virgil *Aeneid* 6.258 (*procul o, procul este, profani*). The two sisters of Agaue were Ino and Autonoe.

714–15 There is striking anaphora here of *ille...ille* and note also the way the word *aper* is picked up in the following line – a device known as epanalepsis (used again with *trepidum* in lines 716–17). *maximus* is a neat touch: the word denotes the pride of the killer in the size of her victim, it is appropriate as this 'boar' was the size of a man and so was 'huge' in boar terms, and its position within the relative clause helps to show the distracted state of Agaue's mind. In Euripides *Bacchae* the crazed Bacchants think that Pentheus is a lion. Agaue here is claiming the right to strike the beast (the gerundive *mihi feriendus* denoting 'is mine to strike') and this notion of possession picks up *nostris* from the line before: the boar is wandering in 'our' fields and so 'I' must strike it. The irony of this whole scene rests on the fact that the women see Pentheus as a vicious animal and kill 'it' in animalistic frenzy themselves. Who is the 'real' animal here?

715–16 The rapid reactions of the women are well suggested by the dactylic rhythm of these lines; the enjambement throughout – as the story rushes over the end of one line into the next just as the mad crowd of women hurtle towards Pentheus – is striking, as is the emphatic word *furens* postponed to the end of the sentence. The hapless Pentheus may be a king but he is all alone (*unum*) as he faces the charging crowd (*turba*). *furor* is usually translated 'madness' and often has the key sense of 'hallucinating' as Agaue is doing here: cf. Hercules who killed his children thinking that they were the children of his enemy, chillingly shown in Seneca's play *Hercules Furens* and in Euripides' *Heracles*.

716 The alliteration of *cunctae coeunt* and assonance of –*umque sequuntur* make this a memorable line; but the repetition of *trepidum* is less effective and possibly Tarrant is correct in reading *fremituque* ('with a roar') in this line in place of *trepidumque*.

717–18 The repetition *iam…iam…iam…iam* is very effective; the pair of lines forms a neat symmetrical couplet, with each line containing the word *iam* twice. There is effective variation of vocabulary with three 'speaking' words (*loquentem…damnantem…fatentem*) with different senses ('speaking', 'condemning', 'confessing') each showing another stage in his demise and all agreeing with an understood *eum*. 'Condemning himself' is similar in meaning to 'admitting that he had done wrong' and the double phrase here shows Ovid's skill in repeating a point without tedious repetition of terms, the repetition showing Pentheus' own repeated protestations of his guilt. There is a notable slowing of the narrative pace in line 718, with its preponderance of spondaic heavy syllables as the poet lingers on the figure of the king trembling as he realises his sin and his doom – and notice the sly touch of *verba minus violenta* (he's not threatening now!).

719 *saucius* is concessive: he was injured but he could still speak. *matertera* is the correct term for one's mother's sister, used here by Pentheus as additional leverage in his appeal ('you are my *aunt…*') as well as calling her by her name in the next line.

720 Pentheus now appeals to the family tree; 'let the shades of Actaeon move your feelings'. Actaeon was the son of Autonoe killed

by his own hounds as his punishment for seeing the goddess Diana bathing naked, a tale narrated in this book (131–252). Pentheus is appealing to a bereaved mother not to kill her nephew.

721 The women are in a state of *ecstasis* induced by the god and are unaware of anything; Autonoe does not know who Actaeon is, any more than Agaue recognises her son Pentheus in front of her. The verb *sit* is missed from the indirect question *nescit quis Actaeon [sit]*. There is a shocking end to the sentence: Pentheus extends his right hand in supplication to her and she rips it off, the violent sudden action well shown in the placing of *abstulit* at the start of the next line in enjambement; Ino then joins in and rips off the other hand.

722 *Inous* is an adjective meaning 'belonging to Ino' and so is to be taken with *raptu* ('by Ino's seizing of it'). *lacero* is a powerful verb, showing the bloody dismembering which was taking place.

723 Just as the sailor-turned-dolphin 'had no arms' (680) so now Pentheus is without arms with which to supplicate his mother as his aunts have taken them both off him – the slowness of his movement brought out by the spondaic rhythm of *infelix quae matri*. The adjective *infelix* ('unfortunate') is a massive understatement but here points the contrast between his arrogant cruelty earlier towards Acoetes and his current situation.

724 Pentheus shows his mother his bleeding stumps (literally 'his amputated wounds') now that his real limbs (*membris*) had been thrown down (*deiectis*, the phrase being an ablative absolute explaining how he came to be mutilated).

725 For all his sickening injuries, Pentheus can utter what are his last words – 'look, mother' – a phrase which is pathetic and sadly moving.

The theme of 'look' in *aspice* is at once picked up as Agaue whooped at 'what she saw' (*visis*). *ululavit* is again onomatopoeic and denotes not shrieks of horror as would be expected but rather the ritual cries of the ecstatic worshipper as at 706.

726 Agaue tossed her head backwards and shook her hair wildly, as Bacchants often do in literature and art (e.g. Catullus 64.255, Euripides *Bacchae* 864–5, Aristophanes *Lysistrata* 1312, E. R. Dodds *The Greeks and the Irrational* (University of California Press, 1968) 273–4). The line is framed by *colla...crinem* ('neck...hair') and the two strong verbs are juxtaposed for violent effect (*iactavit movitque*).

727 Pentheus has now been decapitated. We are not shown the act but here his mother holds his 'torn-off head' in an 'embrace' (*complexa*) which is apt for mother and son but which is chillingly ironic in this context. Her fingers are 'blood-stained' (*cruentis*) which is as near as we get to Ovid telling us that she had done the decapitating.

728 *opus hoc* is in apposition to *victoria nostra*: 'this deed represents victory for us'. She addresses her sisters and fellow-worshippers as *comites* (literally 'companions').

729–31 Ovid stresses the power of the god one last time here with his simile comparing the ease with which Pentheus' limbs were stripped off him with the ease with which nature strips leaves off trees in autumn. The leaves are described in some detail – they are 'touched by the cold of autumn', finding it hard to cling on to their position high up on a tree – when they are summarily dispatched from their tree in three short words at the end of line 730. *non citius*, 'no more quickly' – i.e. 'just as quickly do...', and *male* has the sense of 'only just'. The simile of leaves falling in autumn is a stock one – cf. Homer *Iliad* 6.146–9, Virgil *Aeneid* 6.309–10 – but here is used differently. The image is standard for the shortness and inevitable end of all human life, but there is nothing inevitable about Pentheus' limbs falling off his body and the moral being pointed is that he was the architect of his own untimely demise. The precise comparison is here between the ease with which a wind can pull off leaves and the ease, with which a Bacchant can pull off the limbs of a man, showing the power of the god. The final word is however highly charged: *nefandus* means 'unspeakable' (derived from *ne* + *fandus* ('not to be spoken')) and is here applied to the 'abominable' hands of the women dismembering Pentheus. This is perhaps surprising as the women were simply obeying the commands of the god who sent them into the trance, and obeying gods is usually regarded as the right thing to do, and perhaps suggests that the *exemplis* in the next line are more 'warnings' than 'models' and that the tone of the ending of the book is the need to bow before the power of the god or risk being either the agent or the victim of his wicked force.

732–3 *exemplis* suggests either models of behaviour or else punishments designed to deter any future misbehaviour, and the 'moral' here is stark realism rather than any cosy theodicy. Ismenus is a river, which flows near Thebes, and so the 'Ismenides' are the Theban women – the word is one which Ovid uses three times in the *Metamorphoses*. The rites are *nova* which recalls Tiresias' prophecy (520) of a *novus Liber* ('a new Bacchus') coming to Thebes and Pentheus' sneering at the *moris novi* in line 581, as well as the description of the *ignota...sacra* in line 530. Just as Acoetes learned from the events he witnessed and ended up saying *sacra frequento* (line 691) so here the women *sacra frequentant*. *tura dant* means that they 'make offerings of incense' and the final couplet stresses above all the acceptance of the sacredness of Bacchus and his rites (*sacra... sanctasque colunt...aras*).

Vocabulary

a, ab (+ *ablative*) away from, by

absisto, absistere, abstiti stand aside, withdraw

abstraho, abstrahere, abstraxi, abstractum draw, drag away

absum, abesse, afui be away, be absent

absumo, absumere, absumpsi, absumptum take away, consume

accedo, accedere, accessi, accessum approach, join (*intransitive*)

accipio, accipere, accepi, acceptum receive

acer, acris, acre eager, fierce

Achais, Achaidis Greek, Achaean

Acoetes, -is Acoetes

Acrisius, -i Acrisius

Actaeon, -onis Actaeon

actutum (*adverb*) immediately

ad (+ *accusative*) to, towards

addisco, addiscere, addidici learn in addition

adduco, adducere, adduxi, adductum draw towards

adimo, adimere, ademi, ademptum take away

aditus, aditus (*m*) entrance, approach

adiuro, adiurare, adiuravi, adiuratum swear by

admiror, admirari, admiratus sum wonder at, admire

admoneo, admonere, admonui, admonitum advise, suggest

admonitus, admonitus (*m*) reminder, warning

adsum, adesse, adfui be present, appear, be there for somebody

aduncus, -a, -um bent, curved

advena, -ae (*m or f*) stranger

adverto, advertere, adverti, adversum turn towards

aequor, aequoris (*n*) sea

aer, aeris (*m*) air

aes, aeris (*n*) bronze

aetas, aetatis (*f*) age, generation

Aethalion, Aethalion (one of Acoetes' sailors)

aether, aetheris (*m*) heavens, air

affero, afferre, attuli, allatum bring to

Agaue, -es Agaue (mother of Pentheus)

ager, agri (*m*) field, land
agito, agitare, agitavi, agitatum drive, brandish
agmen, agminis (*n*) band, column
ago, agere, egi, actum drive, do, accomplish, spend time
ait he says, he said
albeo, albere be white
Alcimedon, -onis Alcimedon (one of Acoetes' sailors)
aliquis, aliquis, aliquid someone, something
aliquis, aliqua, aliquid some
aliter otherwise, in another way
alius, alia, aliud other
alter, alterius one or other of two
altus, -a, -um high, tall
ambages, ambagis (*f*) round-about way, confusion, ambiguity
amens, amentis mad, distraught
amor, amoris (*m*) love
anguigenus, -a, -um born of a snake or dragon
animus, -i (*m*) mind, courage, spirit
antemna, -ae (*f*) sailyard, sail
aper, apri (*m*) wild boar
appello, appellare, appellavi, appellatum call
applico, applicare, applicavi, applicatum bring near to, bring to land
aptus, -a, -um fitting, suitable
aqua, -ae (*f*) water
ara, -ae (*f*) altar
arbor, arboris (*f*) tree
Arctos, -i Arctos (constellation of the Great Bear)
Argolicus, -a, -um belonging to Argos
arma, armorum (*n pl*) weapons
ars, artis (*f*) skill, art
arvum, -i (*n*) field
aspergo, asperginis (*f*) sprinkling, spray
aspicio, aspicere, aspexi, aspectum, see, look at
assumo, assumere, assumpsi, assumptum take, gain, claim
at but
Athamas, -antis Athamas (a Theban)
attono, attonare, attonui, attonitum thunder at, stupefy

attraho, attrahere, attraxi, attractum draw towards
audax, audacis bold
audio, audire, audivi, auditum hear
aufero, auferre, abstuli, ablatum carry off, take away
augur, auguris (*m or f*) soothsayer, prophet
auguror, augurari, auguratus sum (*deponent*) prophesy, foretell
aura, -ae (*f*) breeze
auris, -is (*f*) ear
Aurora, -ae (*f*) (goddess of) Dawn
aurum, -i (*n*) gold
Autonoe, -es (*f*) Autonoe (mother of Actaeon and aunt of Pentheus)
autumnus, -i (*m*) autumn
avello, avellere, avulsi, avulsum tear off
avus, -i (*m*) grandfather

Bacchicus, -a, -um of Bacchus
bacchor, bacchari, bacchatus sum to revel as a Bacchant
Bacchus, -i the god Bacchus
bellicus, -a, -um warlike, military
bellum, -i (*n*) war
bracchium, -ii (*n*) arm
brevis, -e short

caecus, -a, -um blind
caedes, caedis (*f*) slaughter
calamus, -i (*m*) reed, fishing-rod
campus, -i (*m*) plain
canorus, -a, -um singing, melodious
cantus, -us (*m*) song
canus, -a, um white, grey
capella, -ae she-goat
capio, capere, cepi, captum capture
caput, capitis (*n*) head
careo, carere, carui, caritum (+ *ablative*) lack
carina, -ae (*f*) ship, boat
catena, -ae (*f*) chain
cauda, -ae (*f*) tail

celo, celare, celavi, celatum hide

census, -us (*m*) wealth, possessions

cerno, cernere, crevi, cretum see, discern

ceterus, -a, -um the rest

Chius, -a, -um belonging to Chios (an island in the Aegean Sea)

chorus, -i (*m*) dance

cingo, cingere, cinxi, cinctum surround, encircle

circa around

circumdo, -dare, -dedi, -datum surround, enwrap

Cithaeron, -onis (*m*) Mount Cithaeron

cito swiftly

citus,-a, -um swift

clades, -is (*f*) disaster

clamo, clamare, clamavi, clamatum shout

clamor, -oris (*m*) shout

clarus, -a, -um clear, bright, loud

claudo, claudere, clausi, clausum close, enclose

coeo, coire, coii, coitum come together, meet, gather

coepi, coepisse, coeptum begin

cognosco, cognoscere, cognovi, cognitum get to know, find out

cogo, cogere, coegi, coactum compel, drive together

collum, -i (*n*) neck

colo, colere, colui, cultum cultivate, worship, cherish

comes, comitis (*m or f*) companion

comminiscor, comminisci, commentus sum invent, feign

complector, complecti, complexus sum embrace

concieo, conciere, concivi, concitum stir, urge, rouse

conscendo, conscendere, conscendi, conscensum climb

consumo, consumere, consumpsi, consumptum devour, spend

contemno, contemnere, contempsi, contemptum despise

contemptor, -oris (*m*) despiser

contingo, contingere, contigi, contactum touch, reach, befall

cor, cordis (*n*) heart

cornu, -us (*n*) horn

corona, -ae (*f*) garland

corpus, corporis (*n*) body

corripio, corripere, corripui, correptum seize, take up, snatch

corymbus, -i (*m*) cluster of berries
credo, credere, credidi, creditum (+ *dative of person*) believe
creo, creare, creavi, creatum create
cresco, crescere, crevi, cretum grow
crimen, criminis (*n*) charge, fault
crinis, crinis (*m*) hair
crucio, cruciare, cruciavi, cruciatum torture, torment
crudelis, -e cruel
cruentatus, -a, -um bloodstained
cruentus, -a, -um bloody
cultus, -us (*m*) appearance, dress
cum when, since, although
cunctus, -a, -um all
cupido, cupidinis (*f*) desire
cupio, cupire, cupii (*or* **cupivi**)**, cupitum** desire
cur why
curro, currere, cucurri, cursum run
cursus, -us running, course
curvamen, curvaminis (*n*) curve, bending
cutis, -is (*f*) skin

damno, damnare, damnavi, damnatum condemn
de (+ *ablative*) down from, about
decet (+ *accusative*) it befits, it is suitable
decipio, decipere, decepi, deceptum deceive
decurro, decurrere, de(cu)curri, decursum run down
decus, decoris (*n*) glory, beauty, honour
deduco, deducere, deduxi, deductum draw down, unfurl
defero, deferre, detuli, delatum bring down, take
deicio, deicere, deieci, deiectum throw down
Delos, -i (*accusative* **Delon**) Delos (island in the Aegean)
demens, dementis mad, foolish
demitto, demittere, demisi, demissum send down
denique finally, at length
deripio, deripere, deripui, dereptum tear off, remove
desertus, -a, -um deserted
desilio, desilire, desilui leap down

deus, dei (*m*) god
dextra, -ae (*f*) right hand
Dia, -ae Dia (alternative name for island of Naxos)
dico, dicere, dixi, dictum say
dictum, -i (*n*) word
Dictys Dictys (one of Acoetes' sailors)
dies, diei (*m or f*) day
differo, differre, distuli, dilatum separate, postpone
digitus, -i (*m*) finger
dignor, dignari, dignatus sum deign, think worthy
diripio, diripere, diripui, direptum snatch away
diruo, diruere, dirui, dirutum tear apart, destroy
dirus, -a, -um dreadful, terrible
distinguo, distinguere, distinxi, distinctum separate, distinguish,
  decorate
diu for a long time
diversus, -a, -um contrary, different
dividuus, -a, -um half
do, dare, dedi, datum give
documentum, -i (*n*) evidence, lesson
dominus, -i (*m*) master
domus, us (*f*) house
dubito, dubitare, dubitavi, dubitatum hesitate, doubt
duco, ducere, duxi, ductum lead
dum while, until
duro, durare, duravi, duratum harden
durus, -a, -um hard
dux, ducis (*m*) leader

e (+ *ablative*) from out of
ecce look!
Echion, -onis Echion (father of Pentheus)
Echionides, -ae The son of Echion (i.e. Pentheus)
edo, edere, edidi, editum give out, utter
efflo, efflare, efflavi, efflatum blow out
ego I
eligo, eligere, elegi, electum select, choose

emergo, emergere, emersi, emersum come out, emerge

en look!

enim for

ensis, -is (*m*) sword

eo, ire, ii, itum go

Epopeus Epopeus (one of Acoetes' sailors)

equus, -i (*m*) horse

erro, errare, erravi, erratum go wrong, err

et and

evenio, evenire, eveni, eventum turn out, come true

ex (+ *ablative*) from out of

excutio, excutere, excussi, excussum shake off

exemplum, -i (*n*) example

exileo, exilire, exilui leap out

exilium, -i (*n*) exile

expleo, explere, explevi, expletum fill, complete

exprimo, exprimere, expressi, expressum push out

exsurgo, exsurgere, exsurrexi rise

facies, -ei (*f*) face, form, appearance

facio, facere, feci, factum do, make

factum, -i (*n*) deed

falcatus, -a, -um curved, sickle-shaped

fallax, fallacis deceiving, false

fallo, fallere, fefelli, falsum deceive

fama, -ae (*f*) report, fame, rumour

famulus, -i (*m*) servant, attendant

fateor, fateri, fassus sum confess, acknowledge

fatum, -i (*n*) fate, destiny

faveo, favere, favi, fautum (+ *dative*) favour

felix, felicis happy, fortunate

femineus, -a, -um womanly

fere nearly, approximately

ferio, ferire strike

fero, ferre, tuli, latum bear, carry

ferrum, -i (*n*) iron

ferus, -a, -um wild, savage

fervens, ferventis ardent, keen, boiling
festus, -a, -um merry, festive
fides, fidei (*f*) faith, pledge
fio, fieri, factus sum become, am made
firmo, firmare, firmavi, firmatum strengthen, confirm
flavus, -a, -um blonde, yellow
flecto, flectere, flexi, flexum bend
fleo, flere, flevi, fletum weep
foedo, foedare, foedavi, foedatum stain, defile
fons, fontis (*m*) spring, source
fore (= futurum esse) to be about to be
foris, -is (*f*) door
forma, -ae (*f*) shape, beauty
forte by chance
fortis, -e brave, strong
fraus, fraudis (*f*) deceit, trick
fremitus, -us (*m*) roaring, shouting
fremo, fremere, fremui, fremitum roar, resound
frequento, frequentare, frequentavi, frequentatum celebrate, throng
frigus, frigoris (*n*) cold
frons, frondis (*f*) leaf
frons, frontis (*f*) brow, forehead
frustra in vain
funis, funis (*m*) rope
furo, furere rage, be furious
furor, furoris (*m*) madness, frenzy

galea, -ae (*f*) helmet
gelidus, -a, -um icy cold
geminus, -a, -um twin, twofold
gens, gentis (*f*) nation, race
gloria, -ae (*f*) glory
gradus, -us (*m*) step, gait
gravidus, -a, -um heavy, pregnant
gravis, -is heavy, serious
grex, gregis (*m*) flock, crowd
guttur, gutturis (*n*) throat

habeo, habere, habui, habitum have, hold
hac...hac... here...here...
haereo, haerere, haesi, haesum stick, cling to
hamus, -i (*m*) hook
harena, -ae (*f*) sand
hasta, -ae (*f*) spear
haud not
hedera, -ae (*f*) ivy
heres, heredis (*m*) heir
hic, haec, hoc this
hic here
honor, honoris (*m*) honour
hortator, -oris (*m*) encourager
hospita, -ae (*f*) friendly
huc to this place
humilis, -is low, poor
Hyades, -um (*f pl*) Hyades – a constellation in Taurus

iaceo, iacere, iacui lie down
iacto, iactare, iactavi, iactatum toss, hurl, boast
iam by now, already
iamdudum for a long time past
ibi there
icio, icere, ici, ictum strike
idem, eadem, idem the same
ignis, -is (*m*) fire
ignotus, -a, -um unknown
ille, illa, illud that
immitto, immittere, immisi, immissum send into
immurmuro, immurmurare murmur at
impedio, impedire, impedi(v)i, impeditum prevent, hinder
impello, impellere, impuli, impulsum push, drive
impero, imperare, imperavi, imperatum (+ *dative*) order, command
impius, -a, -um unholy, wicked
inanis, -e empty, unreal
incipio, incipere, incepi, inceptum begin
increpo, increpare, increpui, increpitum blame, reproach

inermis, -e unarmed
infelix, infelicis unhappy, unfortunate
infero, inferre, intuli, illatum bring in
ingens, ingentis huge
inhibeo, inhibere, inhibui, inhibitum restrain, check
inludo, inludere, illusi, illusum mock, jeer, play at
Inous, -a, -um of or belonging to Ino (aunt of Pentheus)
inquit he said
inrito, inritare, inritavi, inritatum excite, arouse
insania, -ae (*f*) madness
insanus, -a, -um mad
instrumentum, -i (*n*) tool, instrument
intereo, interire, interi(v)i, interitum perish
intexo, intexere, intexui, intextum weave into
intorqueo, intorquere, intorsi, intortum twist, plait
io oh (ritual exclamation)
ipse, ipsa, ipsum himself, herself, itself
ira, -ae (*f*) anger
is, ea, id he, she, it
Ismenis, -idos A Theban woman
iste, ista, istum that
iterum again
iubeo, iubere, iussi, iussum order
iuro, iurare, iuravi, iuratum swear
ius, iuris (*n*) right, power
iuvenalis, -e youthful
iuvenis, -is (*m*) young man
iuvo, iuvare, iuvi, iutum help, delight

labor, laboris (*m*) labour, toil
laboro, laborare, laboravi, laboratum work
lacer, lacera, lacerum torn in pieces
lacero, lacerare, laceravi, laceratum tear in pieces
lacertus, -i (*m*) arm
lacrima-ae (*f*) tear
lacus, -us (*m*) lake, pool
laevus, -a, -um on the left

lascivus, -a, -um playful, wanton
latex, laticis (*m*) water, liquid
latus, -a, um wide, broad
lenis, -e smooth, gentle
letum, -i (*n*) death
levis, -e light
Liber, -Liberi (*m*) Liber (Italian god identified with Bacchus/
Dionysus)
Libys, -uos Libys (one of Acoetes' sailors)
ligo, ligare, ligavi, ligatum bind, tie up
linteum, lintei (*n*) linen, sail
linum, -i (*n*) thread, linen, net
litus, litoris (*n*) shore
locus, -i (*m*) place (*plural* **loca**)
longus, -a, -um long
loquor, loqui, locutus sum speak
ludo, ludere, lusi, lusum play, make fun of
lumen, luminis (*n*) light, eye
luna, -ae (*f*) moon
luo, luere, lui wash, atone for
lux, lucis (*f*) light
Lycabas Lycabas (one of Acoetes' sailors)
lynx, lyncis (*m or f*) lynx

madidus, -a, -um wet, dripping
Maeonia, -ae (*f*) Maeonia
magicus, -a, -um magic
maior (*comparative form of* magnus) – greater
male badly
manus, -us (*f*) hand, band of men
mare, -is (*n*) sea
Mars, Martis Mars (god of war)
mater, matris (*f*) mother
matertera, -ae (*f*) aunt
Mavortius, -a, -um of Mars
maximus, -a, -um (*superlative form of* magnus) greatest
medius, -a, -um middle, midst of

Medon Medon (one of Acoetes' sailors)

Melanthus, -i Melanthus (one of Acoetes' sailors)

membrum, -i (*n*) limb

memor, memoris mindful of

mens, mentis (*f*) mind

mereo, merere, merui, meritum deserve

merum, -i (*n*) unmixed wine

metus, -us (*m*) fear

meus, mea, meum my

mille a thousand

ministerium, -ii (*n*) job, task, office

minus less

miraculum, -i (*n*) wonder, marvel

miror, mirari, miratus sum I am amazed at

misceo, miscere, miscui, mixtum mix

miser, misera, miserum wretched, sad

mitto, mittere, misi, missum send

moderamen, -aminis (*n*) restraint, steering

modero, moderare, moderavi, moderatum regulate, control

modicus, -a, -um moderate

modo only; just now

modus, -i manner, measure

moenia, -ium (*n pl*) walls of a city

mollis, -e soft, effeminate

moneo, monere, monui, monitum warn, advise

mons, montis (*f*) mountain

monstro, monstrare, monstravi, monstratum show, point out

mora, -ae (*f*) delay

morior, mori, mortuus sum die

mors, mortis (*f*) death

mortalis, -e mortal

mos, moris (*m*) custom, rites, usage

moveo, movere, movi, motum move

mox soon

multus, -a, -um much, many

murra, -ae (*f*) myrrh

namque for

nanciscor, nancisci, nactus sum find, obtain

naris, -is (*f*) nostril, nose

natus, -i (*m*) son

nauta, -ae (*m*) sailor

navale, -is (*n*) dockyard

Naxos, -i (*f*) Naxos (island in the Aegean, also called Dia)

ne lest, not to…

nefandus, -a, -um unspeakable, abominable

nego, negare, negavi, negatum deny, say that…not

neque and not, nor

nescio, nescire, nesci(v)i, nescitum do not know

nex, necis (*f*) violent death

nexus, -us (*m*) coil, entwining

nigresco, nigrescere, nigrui grow black

nihil nothing

nil (*shortened form of* **nihil**)

nimium too much

nisi unless, if…not

noceo, nocere, nocui, nocitum (+ *dative*) harm, hurt

nomen, nominis (*n*) name

non not

noster, nostra, nostrum our

noto, notare, notavi, notatum mark, observe

novissimus, -a, -um most recent

novus, -a, -um new, strange

nox, noctis (*f*) night

nullus, -a, -um none, not any

numen, numinis (*n*) divine power

numerus, -i (*m*) number

nunc now

nurus, -us (*f*) daughter-in-law

nutus, -us (*m*) nod

o o!

obex, obicis (*m or f*) bar, obstruction

obicio, obicere, obieci, obiectum throw at, taunt with

obscenus, -a, -um ill-omened, impure

obsisto, obsistere, obstiti oppose, stand before

obsto, obstare, obstiti (+ *dative*) hinder, resist

obstruo, obstruere, obstruxi, obstructum put in the way

obstupesco, obstupescere, obstipui be astounded

obverto, obvertere, obverti, obversum turn up, turn inwards

ocior, ocius swifter

oculus, -i (*m*) eye

Olenius, -a, -um Olenian (referring to the star Capella associated
  with Aege daughter of Olenus)

omnis, -e all

ops, opis (*f*) help (*plural*: wealth, resources)

Opheltes Opheltes (one of Acoetes' sailors)

opus, operis (*n*) work, task

ora, -ae (*f*) shore, edge

orbus, -a, -um (+ *genitive*) bereaved of, lacking

ostendo, ostendere, ostendi, ostensum show

pampineus, -a, -um made of vine tendrils

pandus, -a, -um curved, bent

panthera, -ae (*f*) panther

parens, parentis (*m*) parent

paro, parare, paravi, paratum prepare

pars, partis (*f*) part

pateo, patere, patui lie open, be revealed

pater, patris (*m*) father

paternus, -a, -um fatherly

patria, -ae (*f*) fatherland

patrius, -a, -um fatherly

patulus, -a, -um broad, spreading

pauper, pauperis poor

pavidus, -a, -um fearful, trembling

pecco, peccare, peccavi, peccatum do wrong

pectus, pectoris (*n*) chest, breast

pello, pellere, pepuli, pulsum drive

penates, -ium (*n pl*) household gods

Pentheus (*accusative* **Penthea**) Pentheus (king of Thebes)
per through
perdo, perdere, perdidi, perditum lose, destroy
pereo, perire, perii perish
perpetior, perpeti, perpessus sum suffer, allow
persequor, persequi, persecutus sum chase after, pursue
persto, perstare, perstiti persist, carry on
pervenio, pervenire, perveni, perventum come to, reach
peto, petere, peti(v)i, petitum seek
pingo, pingere, pinxi, pictum paint, embroider
pinna, -ae (*f*) fin
pinus, -us (*f*) pine, ship
piscis, -is (*m*) fish
plebs, plebis (*f*) common people
pluvialis, -e rainy
poena, -ae (*f*) punishment, penalty
pondus, ponderis (*n*) weight
pono, ponere, posui, positum place, put aside
pontus, -i (*n*) sea
porta, -ae (*f*) gate
portus, -us (*f*) port, harbour
possum, posse, potui can, be able
post after, behind
praebeo, praebere, praebui, praebitum offer, give
praeceps, praecipitis headlong
praeda, -ae (*f*) booty, spoils
praesagus, -a, -um prophetic
praesens, praesentis present, powerful
praeter (+ *accusative*) except, besides
precor, precari, precatus sum pray
prehendo, prehendere, prehendi, prehensum grasp
primo at first
primus, -a, -um first
pro (+ *ablative*) for, on behalf of, instead of
probo, probare, probavi, probatum approve
procer, proceris (*m*) chief
procul far from

profanus, -a, -um unholy, uninitiated
profugus, -a, -um exiled
proles, prolis (*f*) offspring
promitto, promittere, promisi, promissum promise
prope near to
propero, properare, properavi, properatum hurry
prora, -ae (*f*) prow
Proreus Proreus (one of Acoetes' sailors)
prospecto, prospectare, prospectavi, prospectatum look out on
prospicio, prospicere, prospexi, prospectum look out
protinus immediately
proturbo, proturbare, proturbavi, proturbatum push away
pudor, pudoris (*m*) shame
puer, -i (*m*) boy
pugna, -ae (*f*) fight, battle
pugnus, -i (*m*) fist
puppis, -is (*f*) (stern of) ship
purpura, -ae (*f*) purple cloth
purus, -a, -um clean, pure
puto, putare, putavi, putatum think

quacumque wherever
quaero, quaerere, quaesivi, quaesitum ask, seek
qualis, -e what sort of
quam how, than
quamquam although
quamvis although
-que and
queror, queri, questus sum complain
qui who
quid what
quidam a certain
quidem indeed
quis? who?
quisque each
quisquis whoever
quo to where

quondam once, at some time
quoque also

rabies, -ei (*f*) madness, rage
racemifer, -a, um cluster-bearing
rapio, rapere, rapui, raptum seize, carry off
rapto, raptare, raptavi, raptatum seize violently
raptus, -us (*m*) carrying off
ratis, -is (*f*) boat
recandesco, recandescere, recandui grow white hot
recens, recentis new, fresh
recurvus, -a, -um bent back, curved
redeo, redire, redii I go back, return
refero, referre, rettuli, relatum bring back, relate
regimen, regiminis (*n*) rudder
relabor, relabi, relapsus sum slide, slip back
relinquo, relinquere, reliqui, relictum leave behind
removeo, removere, removi, remotum remove
remus, -i (*m*) oar
repandus, -a, -um bent back, crooked
repello, repellere, reppuli, repulsum drive back
repeto, repetere, repeti(v)i, repetitum seek again
requies, requietis (*f*) rest
res, rei (*f*) thing, matter
resilio, resilire, resilui leap back
responsum, -i (*n*) response, reply
resto, restare, restiti stand still, remain
retendo, retendere, retendi, retentum loosen, unbend
retineo, retinere, retinui, retentum hold back, check
rictus, -i (*m*) gaping jaws
rideo, ridere, risi, risum laugh, laugh at
rogo, rogare, rogavi, rogatum ask
roro, rorare, roravi, roratum be wet, run with
rubesco, rubescere, rubui grow red
rudens, rudentis (*m*) rope
rumpo, rumpere, rupi, ruptum break, shatter
ruo, ruere, rui, rutum rush

rursus back again

sacer, -cra, -crum sacred, holy
sacrum, -i (*n*) rite, sacrifice
saevus, -a, -um savage
salio, salire, salui leap
saltus, -us (*m*) leap, jump
salus, salutis (*f*) safety
sanguis, sanguinis (*m*) blood
satis enough
saucius, -a, -um wounded
saxum, -i (*n*) rock
scelus, sceleris (*n*) crime
scilicet of course, doubtless
scopulus, -i (*m*) rock, cliff
se himself, herself, themselves
sed but
sedes, sedis (*f*) seat, abode
segnis, -e late, sluggish, slow
Semeleius, -a, -um belonging to Semele
semper always
senex, senis (*m*) old man
sensus, -us (*m*) sense, feeling
sentio, sentire, sensi, sensum feel, perceive
sequor, sequi, secutus sum follow
serpens, serpentis (*m or f*) dragon, snake
serpo, serpere, serpsi, serptum creep, wind
si if
sic thus
siccus, -a, -um dry
sidus, sideris (*n*) star
significo, significare, significavi, significatum make known, reveal
signum, -i (*n*) sign
silva, -ae (*f*) forest, wood
similis, -e like
simulacrum, -i (*n*) image, likeness
sine without

sino, sinere, sivi, situm allow
sinuo, sinuare, sinuavi, sinuatum wind, bend, curve
sisto, sistere, steti/stiti halt, cease
sive...sive whether...or
socius, -i (*m*) ally
soleo, solere, solitus sum be accustomed to
solidus, -a, -um solid, strong
solus, -a, -um alone
solvo, solvere, solvi, solutum loosen, set free
somnus, -i (*m*) sleep
sono, sonare, sonui, sonitum make a sound
sopor, soporis (*m*) sleep
soror, sororis (*f*) sister
sors, sortis (*f*) oracle, fate
spargo, spargere, sparsi, sparsum sprinkle, scatter
spatium, -i (*n*) space, extent, length
species, speciei (*f*) appearance, form
spectabilis, -e open to view
specto, spectare, spectavi, spectatum look at, watch
sperno, spernere, sprevi, spretum scorn
spina, -ae (*f*) spine, back
sponte of one's own accord
spumeus, -a, -um foaming
squama, -ae (*f*) scale (on fish)
stirps, stirpis (*f*) race, stock
sto, stare, steti, statum stand
strepitus, -us (*m*) noise, din
stringo, stringere, strinxi, strictum draw (a weapon)
studium, -i (*n*) desire, eagerness, pursuit
Stygius, -a, -um of the river Styx
sub under
subeo, subire, subi(v)i, subitum go under, come up to
successor, -oris (*m*) follower, successor
sum, esse, fui am
summus, -a, -um highest, top of
sumo, sumere, sumpsi, sumptum take up, undertake
superi, -orum (*m pl*) the gods

susurro, susurrare whisper
suus, sua, suum his, her, its

talis, -e such
tam so
tamen however
tamquam as if, just as
tango, tangere, tetigi, tactum touch
tantus, -a, -um so great
Taygete, -es (*accusative* **Taygeten**) Taygete (one of the Pleiades)
tectum, -i (*n*) house, dwelling, roof
tego, tegere, texi, tectum cover, hide
tellus, telluris (*f*) earth, land
telum, -i (*n*) weapon, spear
templum, -i (*n*) temple
tempora, -um (*n pl*) temples, brows
tempto, temptare, temptavi, temptatum attempt, try
tempus, temporis (*n*) time
tendo, tendere, tetendi, tentum stretch
tenebrae, -arum (*f pl*) darkness
teneo, tenere, tenui, tentum hold, steer towards, occupy
tergum, -i (*n*) back
terra, -ae (*f*) land
terreo, terrere, terrui, territum terrify, frighten
Thebae, -arum Thebes
thyrsus, -i (*m*) bacchic wand
tibia, -ae (*f*) pipe
tigris, -is (*m or f*) tiger
timor, timoris (*m*) fear
titubo, titubare, titubavi, titubatum stagger, totter
tormentum, -i (*n*) torture, rack
torrens, torrentis (*m*) torrent
tot so many
totus, -a, -um all of, whole
trabs, trabis (*f*) beam
trado, tradere, tradidi, traditum hand over, give
traho, trahere, traxi, tractum drag

tremendus, -a, -um terrible, frightening
tremo, tremere, tremui tremble
trepidus, -a, -um fearful, scared
truncus, -a, -um limbless, mutilated
tu you (*singular*)
tuba, -ae (*f*) trumpet
tubicen, tubicinis (*m*) trumpeter
tum then
tumulus, -i (*m*) mound
turba, -ae (*f*) crowd
tus, turis (*n*) incense
Tuscus, -a, -um Etruscan
tutela, -ae (*m*) guardian, watcher
tuus, tua, tuum your
tympanum, -i (*n*) drum
Tyros (*accusative* **Tyron**) Tyre (Phoenician city)
Tyrrhenus, -a, -um Etruscan

ubi where, when
udus, -a, -um wet
ultimus, -a, -um last, furthest
ululatus, -us (*m*) howling, wail, shriek
ululo, ululare, ululavi, ululatum howl
umbra, -ae (*f*) shade, shadow, ghost
unda, -ae (*f*) wave
undique on all sides
unus, una, unum one
urbs, urbis (*f*) city
usus, -us (*m*) use
ut so that, when, as, though
utinam would that...
uva, -ae (*f*) grape

vacuus, vacua, vacuum empty, free
vado, vadere go
valeo, valere, valui, valitum be strong, have power
vanus, vana, vanum empty, insubstantial

vates, vatis (*m*) prophet, seer
veho, vehere, vexi, vectum carry, bear
velo, velare, velavi, velatum cover, wrap
velum, -i (*n*) sail
velut(i) as if
venia, -ae pardon
venio, venire, veni, ventum come
ventus, -i (*m*) wind
verber, verberis (*n*) beating, strike
verbum, -i (*n*) word
verto, vertere, verti, versum turn
verus, -a, -um true
vester, vestra, vestrum your (*pl*)
vestis, -is (*f*) clothing
veto, vetare, vetui, vetitum forbid
via, -ae (*f*) road, way
victoria, -ae (*f*) victory
video, videre, vidi, visum see
videor, videri, visus sum seem
viginti twenty
vincio, vincire, vinxi, vinctum bind, tie up
vinco, vincere, vici, victum overcome, conquer
vinum, -i (*n*) wine
violentus, -a, -um violent
violo, violare, violavi, violatum pollute, injure
vir, viri (*m*) man
virgineus, -a, -um girlish
vis, vim, vi (*f*) strength
vix scarcely, with difficulty
voco, vocare, vocavi, vocatum call
volo, velle, volui want
vos you (*pl*)
vox, vocis (*f*) voice
vulgus, -i (*n*) crowd, common folk
vulnus, vulneris (*n*) wound